NAKED WITH THE ENNEAGRAM

A POWERFULLY ACCURATE, NO-BS JOURNEY INTO YOUR UNIQUE PERSONALITY TYPE

ADRIANA TENORA

D1518290

CONTENTS

NAKED WITH THE ENNEAGRAM
PART 2

Dedicated to you my beautiful reader:
May you have the ultimate enlightening self-discovery journey.

FREE GIFTS

To say thank you for buying my book, I would like to give you:

- A **Cheatsheet with a Summary of all the Enneagram Types** — to make remembering and understanding even easier, you can always come back to it in times of need. All the types' main personality traits, worst fear, heart's desire, biggest sin & more at a glance. You can also print it out and pin it somewhere in your home or office where you'll easily see it.
- A high-resolution, printable **Daily Affirmations and Transformations sheet for each Enneagram Type** — to help you quickly recognize old patterns and replace them with a boost of transforming energy through your affirmations for your specific type. Pin them anywhere you can see them daily, at home or at the office; put them on a wall in a nice frame or even save them as a desktop background.
- An **Excel file to automatically calculate the Enneagram test results** — the first test (Test A) is the base test and has the most questions. To make things easier for you, I created an Excel file where

you can insert your scores for Test A and the results will be automatically calculated. There is a specific tab for each test where you can fill in your answers and scores to keep a record of your results.

- A **Summary of the book** *Naked With the Enneagram* — in this pocketbook version you can go over the "CliffsNotes" of the book without going into much detail. Use it as you see fit. For example, as a short read reminder of the complete book, or share the link as a gift to a friend who's not quite ready to embark on the complete book journey, or whatever else helps you.
- High-resolution, printable **Images from the book** *Naked With the Enneagram* — to have a better experience while reading the white & black version of the book all the color images are accessible to view online, download or print. Choose what works best for you.

Download Here:
www.NakedEnneagram.com/freebies
(or scan the QR code at the end of the book)

Some of the information above probably won't make full sense until you go through the book, so you can find this page at the end of this book as well.
Happy Reading.

NAKED WITH THE ENNEAGRAM

PART 1

A Powerfully Accurate, no-BS Journey into Your Unique Personality Type

DON'T LIVE THE LIFE THAT WAS GIVEN TO YOU

"Why do I do the things I do?"

During the toughest periods of my life, I'd ask this question and be met with silence. Whether it was sabotaging a new job or relationship, wasting time feeling not good enough, or letting my fears get the better of me. I felt like I was just repeating subconscious responses to life, without truly understanding why the choices I kept making weren't leading to a point of personal strength or happiness. Instead, it felt like I was losing control... I just couldn't find a way to predict and change my subconscious responses to life — which meant I was stuck in the same repeating patterns, like a broken carnival ride with no exit.

When I discovered the Enneagram, it wasn't love at first sight. I'm not usually the type who believes in astrology or personality tests. I dislike the idea of dividing people into certain boxes (I found out later that the Enneagram actually does the opposite — it shows you how to break free from your box). I always considered myself more of a hard-science type of person. But, since I'm very interested in self-development, I approached it with an open mind.

When I decided to take a peek and see what the Enneagram could do for me, I did it solely on the off-chance of learning something new about myself. It took a while to find my type — if you've taken Enneagram tests online, you might already know how inaccurate they can be. I had to take multiple quizzes because I kept getting different results, and I had to read many books. Because, well, most of the well-structured books out there are just too academic and hard to decipher. Plus, many of them leaned too much toward the negative side of the types (I might be a perfectionist One, but I don't appreciate having my controlling nature shoved in my face every two seconds). I wanted to find a way to recognize my strengths and grow into my own best self, instead of being criticized for what other people see as faults. But, back to the Enneagram.

The more I read, the more I felt *seen*. I realized that most of the arguments I was having with my family and friends were about relatively small things, that for me seemed absolutely fundamental. For example, to not be late without a good reason, or to respect the rules of the house. If someone promised something, no matter how small, and didn't see it through, I would take it very personally (depending on who it was, I might even cut them out of my life completely).

The Enneagram helped me see how critical, demanding, and insensitive I was being. I am a Type 1, by the way, so I guess it figures!

For as long as I can remember, my home had to be immaculate, and God forbid someone were to move something and not put it back in its precise location. Everything had a designated place, and once you were done with it, it must be put back. Even today, after over 20 years, my BFF remembers when we were sharing an apartment and I would give her hell for not keeping the shampoos in order (sorry, Dari, I know better now).

Even though I knew that not everyone saw things the way I do, I still thought I was *right*. The Enneagram finally made me more empathetic and able to understand why other people thought and acted differently, or had other priorities.

I also realized how much time I was losing whenever I had to make a decision, no matter how big or small it was. I over-analyze because of my obsessive perfectionism — I want to be as sure as possible that I'm making the right decision. And I'm the master of lists — I keep files on everything!

These used to be personality traits I treasured, but the Enneagram made me understand how my behaviors created unhealthy patterns that cost me time and affected the quality of my relationships with my loved ones.

I never considered myself weak, but I definitely feel stronger and more confident now that I'm more aware of my own actions. It's like I received external confirmation that this is *who I am*; that someone could see the real me for the first time. Okay, If I'm being totally honest, it was more than just an AHA! moment. It was a real slap in the face that made me get my priorities straight. To all Ones out there, no, having the books on your shelf in no particular order is not missing-a-fun-night-out-worthy.

Discovering my Enneagram type and delving deeper into my traits allowed me to plan clear goals for myself and actually follow through without feeling distracted, overwhelmed, or helpless. It felt like the fog had cleared, the blindfold was removed, and I was finally able to see a clear path leading to personal growth.

It even allowed me to find and deepen a romantic relationship in ways I didn't expect.

My partner is a Type 7. He's not the type to take things seriously unless he has to. He'd spend his days always doing fun stuff if he could — taking on new adventures and making friends. He can start a conversation with anyone, anywhere. Once, we were in the line for a baguette (we currently live in Paris — you have to try an authentic French baguette!), and he just, out of the blue, let the person in front of us know how cool his leather jacket was. It didn't take long to exchange numbers and plan to meet up for drinks later.

Initially, he didn't take lightly to all the days I refused to go out because I was working on this book. And let me tell you, he couldn't have cared less about the Enneagram when I first mentioned it. But since we live together, he also couldn't escape my daily remarks and comments (again, I am a One, after all), and one day he gave in and decided to read more about it for himself. Now I can't stop smiling when I hear him talking to other people and recommending the Enneagram because of the results he achieved for himself.

As I found myself going deeper and deeper in my studies of the Enneagram, I began to get frustrated with the available material. And since the One in me just had to have an all-in-one-place type of Enneagram source, I wrote this book. So, many sleepless nights and tons of adventures with my partner *not* taken (which I promise to make up for, by the way), here I am now, sharing *Naked With the Enneagram* with everyone who wishes to deepen their self-awareness and accelerate personal growth.

If you've ever asked questions like, "How can I have more fulfilling relationships?" or, "How can I achieve better results in my work and live a more satisfying life?" then this book may be the secret key that unlocks everything for you. Want to know what has been keeping you from living the life of your dreams? Well, the Enneagram has all the answers!

If you need a no-nonsense, written-by-a-perfection-addict kind of book that delivers on its promises, then you know what to do. Inside these pages, you will find:

- Clear and concise information about each type
- How to practically apply the Enneagram to your life experience
- Practical integration and application methods, diagrams and explanations of each type
- An introduction to all the important Enneagram concepts: wings, instinctual subtypes, stress and growth lines, levels of development, and centers
- A deeper explanation of the challenges of each type (unlike most short reads), and most importantly, information on how to overcome those challenges
- A dedicated section for self-development for each type
- A dedicated section for spirituality for each type: struggles, life lessons, and the path of integration
- Compatibility between each of the types, as well as how various types are mistaken for each other
- A fun Enneatype quote to share with your friends and family

- A complex test to discover your Enneagram type

What this book's NOT: An over-complicated, academic tone; a philosophical or theological lecture; a boring textbook, lacking actionable steps.

I'm not saying the Enneagram will perform miracles in your life, but it's impossible to walk away without learning something about yourself. Do you want to live a richer, more fulfilling, and happier life? Then keep reading — and discover the naked truth about your Enneagram type and how to tap into your true life potential.

To help you reach this profound self-awareness and find out your Enneagram type, I've also included an in-depth, six-part, super-accurate Enneagram test. Find it in the other part of this book, and embark on this life-changing train. Spoiler alert — self-discovery is your final destination!

CHAPTER 1 - THE MAP TO YOUR HIDDEN SELF

"It's black and royal blue!"

"How can you *say* that?! It's obviously white and gold!"

Remember "the dress"? It was a viral internet sensation, with people hotly debating whether the dress in the picture was black and blue, or white and gold. More than 10 million tweets later, neuroscientists were trying to come up with an explanation for why we saw things so differently.

It all came down to how the brain perceives things.

Now, although the dress example was to do with vision, it teaches us a powerful lesson — we can all be looking at the *same* thing, but see it in totally different ways.

This is the basis of the Enneagram.

The Enneagram gives us the keys to understanding nine different ways of looking at life.

We're all living in the same universe, right?

And yet we all see it totally differently.

We all act differently.

We have different political views, religious beliefs, behaviors, ways of being and thinking, and acting...

At times, it can seem like total chaos. We argue with our partners, each not able to understand the other's point. Religious and political debates turn angry, burning bridges between us and breaking down connections. From small things like friendships drifting apart, to huge things like wars being waged, differences in perspective, and our inability to bridge those gaps can cause pain and destruction.

It's also really easy to judge others who see the world in a different way than we do. They're stupid. They're uneducated. They're too emotional. Their point of view is not relevant. In fact, *they're* not relevant. We may even dehumanize people, refusing to understand where they're coming from at all. Refusing to recognize their contribution.

There's another side to this, too. We can also struggle because *other* people seem to have it all together, to have the success we want, the happiness we want, the sense of wholeness we want. Maybe on your lunch break, you scroll through your Instagram feed and feel pangs of jealousy and think, "Why can't I live the amazing life they do?"

Do you feel unfulfilled in your work? Maybe you go through the same darn routine every day, wondering when your *real* life will finally begin. Many of us are sleepwalking through life, not really feeling awake and alive. Our dreams fade away into nothing. The routine threatens to engulf our soul completely unless we strike out, and this can be in harmful ways, like addiction, affairs, and more. We're trying to recapture the *intensity* of life, but it still eludes us, and in fact, destroys us in the process.

Maybe your relationship has gone totally stale, or you find yourself trapped in one unhealthy relationship after another.

Maybe your life is falling apart. Or perhaps your zest for life is being slowly, slowly, slowly squeezed out of you by boredom and routine, until you feel like nothing more than a shell.

These feelings are so common. Trust me, you're not alone.

But what are we doing wrong?

The Enneagram has the answers.

In this book, you'll find out your Enneagram type and gain a deep understanding of who you really are. You will unravel long-suppressed thoughts and finally understand unexpected feelings and rushes of intense emotions (no, it is not always hormones!). In short, you will get in touch with your true self.

The one that has been masked by years of learning to adapt to the world, accept new experiences, and be okay with things that, deep down, make you uncomfortable.

Your Enneagram type is the map that leads to your hidden self!

With that comes positives and negatives. There are things you're *awesome* at. Each Enneagram type comes with unique gifts. For example, Type Ones do everything by a moral code, and Type Fours are often very creative. But there are also ways your Enneagram type is *totally* holding you back. This is because the way you approach life is limited by your Enneagram type. You can easily get stuck in certain ways of thinking, which can help you in certain areas but have you completely stuck in others.

Understanding your Enneagram type helps you massively. While your type won't change, you *can* learn how to:

1. Embrace your strengths
2. Get to know your weaknesses
3. Take full control over your personality so you can make real progress

Now, there's something we have to talk about.

While at times, studying the Enneagram can be fun and inspiring, at other times, it can be *hard.*

When you read the descriptions of how your type can totally go off the edge, or behave in a toxic way, it doesn't feel good. It feels a little like you're naked and people are looking at you. It's going to make you cringe. It's going to make you feel ashamed. It's going to bring out your deepest fears and your biggest insecurities, and it is going to trigger you!

But underneath all of these unpleasant thoughts and feelings, lies something positive.

Discovering negative parts of your personality is actually a step in the right direction. It's a sign you're being honest with yourself and being open to the process. That's true for most self-development work. The more you can lean into these feelings of discomfort, the quicker you can work through them and come out on the other side.

This process of looking at the parts of ourselves we really don't want to see is sometimes called "Shadow Work." That's a term based on the work of the psychologist Carl Jung.

The *shadow* is an aspect of our personality that is left in the dark — we unconsciously let it remain unseen.

To grasp this even better, think of an object that is illuminated by the light. You can see it well. Its shape, color, lines. But the light also casts a shadow, a part of that object that you cannot see from that point of view. An area of darkness that remains the blind spot. That area represents all of the things that you refuse to acknowledge about your personality and life, in general. Just like with the blind spot, you are completely blind (pun intended!) to some parts of your being.

That blindness represents the difference between who you see yourself as and who you really are.

But the blind spot is not the ugly side of the object (or your personality) by default. Not all of us sweep our bad traits under the carpet. Some people live their lives focused so much on their negative characteristics, that they hide most of their positive qualities in their shadow.

The ultimate goal is to rise from that unconsciousness and unleash our true self. Once we get everything out in the open — both from the illuminated side and the shadow — we can discover and accept our true self.

Carl Jung said, "To become conscious of [the shadow] involves recognizing the dark aspects of the personality as present and real. This act is an essential condition for any kind of self-knowledge."

And this sums up why you can be brave and face your shadow — because there's a reward at the end: self-knowledge.

Once you're armed with self-knowledge, life becomes a *totally* different party. You know what you want, and what you don't want. You're stronger, more confident, more resilient. You say "no" when you mean "no" and "HELL YES!" to your dreams. You realize you don't have time to waste doing things that don't serve your growth. You stop caring what other people think about the choices you make and start *owning* your life from the inside out. You wake up in the morning knowing that, each day, you're taking steps towards your goals and dreams.

Sounds like a good place to be, doesn't it?

The Enneagram can get you there.

This book is going to open the door to self-knowledge. All you have to do is simply walk through it.

Once you enter the other side, you'll be able to see deeply into not only yourself but into others as well. You'll learn why you do the things you do, and how to change what has been holding you back. You'll be able to understand the people around you so much better, which will help you to improve your relationships with them and become closer. It'll give you boundaries, which means under-standing how the way you act affects others and how their actions affect you. It also means putting in place measures so that you don't hurt each other emotionally so much.

You know, some people just see the Enneagram as a personality test.

Trust me, it is *so* much more than that.

It's the key to open the door to the next level of your life. The level where you know what steps to take next to reach true fulfillment and wholeness. And honestly, there's no better feeling in life than knowing who you are and where you're going.

In this book, we're going to dive deep into the Enneagram.

I'm not just going to show you each personality type.

We're going to go deep into the technicalities of the Enneagram — wings, instinctual subtypes, stress and growth lines, levels of development, and centers. Don't worry if you don't know what any of these are. I'm going to break them down so they're really easy to understand. These technical parts of the Enneagram are what really makes you understand everything about yourself. It's actually fascinating, and pretty comforting, to discover that the way you are is *not* random! The way we all act fits into a pattern that the Enneagram describes. It describes you even *when* you change, as well as *how* you change and *why* you change. It describes the moments you act out of character and explains why this happens. Pretty amazing, huh?

Getting to know all of this makes sense of the mystery of being human. And once we understand something, we can work within that system to make positive change. To grow. To become the absolute best version of ourselves, for our own sake, for our own lives.

It's actually very exciting.

Imagine if all of humanity studied the Enneagram. The world would be a much better place because we'd understand ourselves and each other.

I'm super excited to see the results for you by the end of this book. When people study the Enneagram, they make *changes.*

Toxic relationships break up, healthy relationships flourish.

People finally get the confidence to go for the career of their dreams, or finally get that business idea going.

And most importantly, you'll get a total *mindset* shift. Meaning, you'll see everything differently now. It's a little hard to explain, but you'll unlock a new part of your mind that observes yourself, and this is the key to growth. By the end of this book, you'll have a framework that helps you understand and interpret what you think, feel, and how you act. You'll be able to *explain* everything you do and why. Nothing will seem a mystery anymore.

I guarantee that, while you read this book, you'll get a new "voice" in your head, which is you analyzing and evaluating how you operate in life. And it's this analyzing voice that will prompt you to make positive changes. It also enables you to feel calmer, and it stops intense emotions from taking over. And, crucially, it's the voice of *wisdom*. That sets a wiser, safer, and more enjoyable course for your life.

I cannot wait to find out what changes you experience! It's going to be an amazing ride.

Ready? Let's dive in!

CHAPTER 2 - ENNEAGRAM: THE MIRROR THAT REFLECTS THE REAL YOU

Imagine yourself going through a challenging time. A situation in which making a decision is not something to be taken lightly. It is like walking down a path of confusion without a sign to point you in the right direction. All of a sudden, there is a giant mirror blocking your way. You stand in front of it, but you are staring at more than just your reflection. You can actually see deeper — deep into your mind, into the far-flung corners of your soul. You can see your thoughts, feelings, emotions. You are no longer absorbed by them — you see them for what they really are.

That mirror is your Enneagram. It is the mental and emotional space within you where you go to get in touch with who you are.

When you're feeling lost and confused, the Enneagram takes you by the hand and gets you out of that whirlwind. It separates you from the way you think and feel and turns you into a more conscious self-observer.

Why is this important?

Because to change, grow, and make healthy progress, we first need to know and accept who we really are. We need to understand our actions, but most importantly, we need to know why we act that way. Once we are able to truly observe ourselves, it becomes possible for us to consciously choose our behavior, which leads to an effective and happy life.

It is the Enneagram that helps us tame the contrary forces (who we are vs. who we want to be). It gives them names and purposes. It helps us let go and accept.

It feels like an impossible task, I know, but all we need is the Enneagram wisdom for the quest of self-discovery to lead us in a positive direction.

Ready for the ride? Let's see how the Enneagram really works.

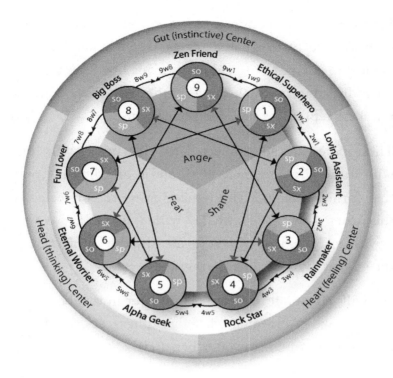

The complete Enneagram diagram

Here's the diagram of the Enneagram. It is *a powerful tool for self-discovery and self-development that can help you reconnect to your true self.* To put it simply, the Enneagram shows nine different types of people and how they interact with each other. Each type has its own way of looking at the world, its own perceptions. Each comes with a unique set of values and things it puts importance on. With different communication and problem-solving styles.

If this seems too complex to you at this point, you can grab a piece of paper and try to sketch it out. Draw a circle and appoint nine numbers (from 1 to 9) in a clockwise direction, with 9 being at the top. Each of these numbers represents a unique Enneagram type.

These types are all connected to each other with lines within the circumference. 9, 3, and 6 are the only ones that form a triangle. The remaining 6 are connected in this order: 1 with 4, 4 with 2, 2 with 8, 8 with 5, 5 with 7, 7 with 1. The shape that is formed by the connection of the 6 types is an irregular hexagram.

We will talk about this connection later in this book, but for the sake of grasping what the Enneagram stands for, knowing its structure is quite beneficial.

Although appointing these numbers seems like a mere classification, know that the Enneagram isn't something that puts a label on our foreheads — it's a tool that helps us grow. We can use the Enneagram to help us free ourselves from destructive patterns and limited thinking. It can help us avoid pitfalls, embrace our strengths, and move into wisdom, understanding, and fulfillment.

It's also really important to say here that one type is not better than another. They all have their own strengths and weaknesses, and all have something unique to contribute.

Around the edge of the diagram, you can see numbers from 1 to 9. These represent different main types. You can only be *one* type, so you can be a 3, but not a 3 and a 9, for instance.

We're going to start exploring the types in depth soon, but here are the personality highlights and behaviors that best explain each type:

Type 1 is moral, perfectionistic, and visionary.
Type 2 is caring, nurturing, and people-oriented.
Type 3 is successful, driven, and image-conscious.
Type 4 is creative, emotionally deep, and self-reflective.
Type 5 is cerebral, academic, and unique in their thinking.
Type 6 is security-conscious, community-oriented, and loyal.
Type 7 is spontaneous, fun-loving, and versatile.
Type 8 is powerful, forceful, and protective.
Type 9 is easy-going, fluid, and peaceful.

You might find that in reading these descriptions, you've narrowed down what *you* could be to two or three options. When you read the in-depth explanations of each type further along in the book, this will really help you work out which one you are. When you read about your type, it's likely you'll feel it in your gut. You might start to feel ashamed, even, or notice the physical senses in your body changing. That's a sure sign you're on the right track. I've also included a detailed test section in the book, so you can be sure of your type.

The first thing to do is to find out your main type out of the 9. But the Enneagram goes much deeper than that. There are not just nine types you can be — there are actually a total of 243 variations you can be. That's right, *two hundred and forty-three!*

First, you can have a dominant *wing*. We're going to talk more about wings later, but what it basically means is that you have strong traits of an Enneagram type that's right next to yours. So let's say you're a Type 7, spontaneous, fun-loving, and versatile, but you also have a very commanding, dominant side, you could be a 7 with an 8 wing, which is written "7w8." This gives us an additional 18 types, bringing us to a total of 27, accounting for the original 9.

Then it goes a level deeper than that. In the Enneagram, there are "instinctual subtypes." These describe the finer distinctions within the same main type. They are basically what happens when the Enneagram main type's *emotional need* merges with one of the three instincts' *instinctual needs*. We'll explore this in more detail later, but the three instincts are:

- Self-preservation (sp)
- Social (so)
- Sexual (sx)

I'll show you later on how each of these looks different, but let's say you've discovered you're a Type 7 with an 8 wing, with a social instinctual subtype. This would be written as "7w8 so."

This brings us to 81 variations.

Some people show two instinctual subtypes. One is dominant, known as the "dominant instinct," while the next is known as the "secondary instinct." The remaining subtype is known as the "blind spot." Let's say you had a social dominant instinct, and self-preservation secondary instinct, while your sexual instinct was your blind spot. This would be written as so/sp. So with our above example of a Type 7 with an 8 wing, you'd be a 7w8 so/sp.

These are the available combinations:

- sp/so
- sp/sx
- so/sp
- so/sx
- sx/sp
- sx/so

Multiplying this by the 27 types and wings, this brings us to a total of 243!

Now, back to the diagram. You may be wondering what all the lines mean. They're not just a pretty pattern. They actually hold a very deep significance that can totally transform the way you see yourself. They explain where we go to in times of stress and in times of growth. They show how we act in different situations, revealing the complexity of our characters. But more on that later. First, let's look at where the Enneagram came from.

MYSTICAL ORIGINS

The history of the Enneagram is shrouded in mystery. No one quite knows where it truly came from, or who first created it.

It's thought that the Enneagram has been passed through Mystery Schools or Secret Societies that study the mysteries of life and the universe, and advanced spirituality. Some people believe the Enneagram has come through Sufi roots — Sufis being mystics that work with Islam. Others think it was started by Christian mystics, who studied the secret inner teachings that required higher levels of knowledge and insight to grasp than regular Christian teachings.

Some still trace it back even further, saying that it originated way back in Ancient Greece. Pythagoras, who today we most often associate with the triangle, practiced mystical mathematics with his followers, dubbed the Pythagoreans. They believed that numbers were the very foundation of the universe and creation, and so to unlock the secrets of the world and human life, they had to study numbers in depth. This also included studying shapes, colors, and sizes of objects, and how that related to mathematics.

Some even go back further than that, linking the Enneagram to the Ancient Egyptian Ennead. The Ennead was a group of nine deities worshipped in Ancient Egypt, and this is maybe the first example of nine being a very significant number. So significant, that the human personality can be divided into *nine* categories or types on the Enneagram.

YOUR UNIQUE PATH

You should be able to see from all this that the Enneagram crosses many religions and traditions, and can be thought of in a spiritual or non-spiritual way.

Some approaches to the Enneagram are deeply spiritual. Each type has its own spiritual lesson to learn while on Earth, and each has its spiritual gifts. Famous Russian mystic George Gurdjieff used the Enneagram to explain the creation of the universe. He gained knowledge of the Enneagram at a monastery in Afghanistan in the 1920s. It's also used in modern Christianity, sometimes as a spiritual tool.

Other approaches, on the other hand, are not spiritual at all. The Enneagram can show you which career paths you'd thrive in, for example. You can compare two types to see if you're compatible with a friend or lover, and the strengths and weaknesses that the relationship would have. The CIA actually used the Enneagram to profile world leaders at one point, and many top corporations use the Enneagram as part of their hiring process.

The Enneagram can also be looked at from a psychiatric and psychological perspective — how the human mind works. Oscar Ichazo and Claudio Naranjo both interpreted the Enneagram in this way and introduced it to modern psychology.

So, whether you're religious or spiritual or not, you can still gain a great deal from the Enneagram. You can use it as a tool to better understand the whole universe and the human spirit, or you can simply use it to choose a career path or help you understand your personality better. It's really useful in getting an understanding of your mental health, too, and even explains addiction issues.

This is the power of the Enneagram. It can get you to whatever YOUR next level is. It's not a doctrine. It's not a belief system. You don't have to pledge allegiance to any religion or god or even any particular perspective. The Enneagram does not *take* from you, or require anything of you. Instead, it's a gift that you can use in whatever way feels comfortable to you, in whatever way serves you in taking your next step, moving to *your own* personal next level.

With the Enneagram, you can:

- Increase your self-awareness
- Boost your emotional intelligence
- Understand how you think, feel, and act
- Identify patterns in your own behavior
- Identify your blind spots so you can work on them
- Clearly see your pitfalls and how you can avoid them
- Work on your relationship and better relate to your partner
- Help choose a career that suits your temperament, strengths, and talents
- Grow your abilities as a leader
- Gain more self-confidence and self-esteem
- Learn how to get along with others better — your colleagues, friends, family, acquaintances, and more

I can't wait to share its power and insight with you.

But there is more to our personality than just one type of Enneagram. In fact, no one is defined by a *single type.* You cannot be just easy-going or a hardcore perfectionist all the time, right? There will be times when you will let go of the things you're comfortable with or do something completely out of character. And we will discuss below exactly why that happens.

The Enneagram is much deeper than assigning each of us a main type. It actually allows us to see that there is more to the behaviors of our unique personality. It will remain at the core of our character, of course, but it will be deeply affected by instincts or the other types on the Enneagram's circumference.

Confused much? Building the Enneagram diagram step by step, and feature by feature, we will go through each aspect in detail, so we can clarify just what it entails:

- Wings
- Instinctual Subtypes
- Stress and Growth Lines
- Levels of Development
- Centers

2.1 THE WINGS THAT BALANCE THE FLIGHT

Your Enneagram type may show your basic personality traits, but the human mind is far more complex than that. None of us can be goal-oriented or in a creative mood all the time. Sometimes you will find yourself sitting at a crossroad of what you really want and what you think is best, not quite sure which direction to take.

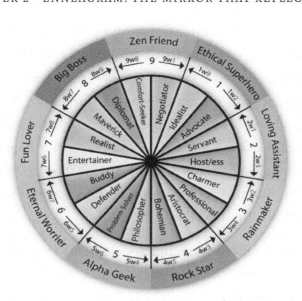

The Wings

Regardless of what your Enneagram type is, we all need some sort of assistance to help us justify the decisions we make. And the Enneagram wings provide just that.

Your wings are other Enneatypes that are placed on either side of your main type. For example, if you're a Type 9, your wings are 8 and 1. For a Type 1, the wings will be 9 and 2, and so on.

Think of the Enneagram wings as the devil and angel sitting on your shoulders. When in doubt, you turn to them for help. *What dress should I wear tonight? How can I slay this work project? What to do about this situation?* And just like you would imagine an angel and devil on your shoulders to do, your Wings will start laying down suggestions and solutions, advising you on how to do the right thing. The trick is that both Wing Types believe they are right. If you are Type 2, you can imagine the perfectionist One and always-aiming-for-the-best Three each pulling you more toward their traits. *Do things in a more organized matter* — Wing 1 would plead. *Just keep pushing until you reach the top* — Wing 3 would scream. It is up to you to decide which one of these Wings has more merit to your personality's needs.

Your wings represent secondary elements to your personality, and you can be more weighted to one than the other, but this will likely change during your life numerous times.

For instance, Type 8s are more aggressive and competitive, and Type 1s are more moralistic and perfectionist. So if you're a Type 9, which is generally laidback and neutral and unemotional, *but* you have the tendency to get very competitive, then you'd be a Type 9 with an 8 wing. This is usually written as "9w8." Other times in your life, you may be very perfectionist, and then you'd be a "9w1."

Some Enneagram experts say that one important goal in self-development is to *balance* your wings. You can do this by taking on activities, careers, or hobbies that nurture each wing. For example, Type 8s love to be physically tough and competitive, so taking on a rough team sport could help a Type 9 get in touch with their 8 wing. On the other hand, Type 1s love causes they can work for to improve the world, so taking on a philanthropic project would help a Type 9 to develop their 1 wing.

When deciding on your main type, if you're struggling to pick between two numbers that are *next* to each other on the Enneagram, so say, 3 and 4, then it's highly likely that one of them is your type and the other is your wing.

A good clue to working out which one is likely to be your main type is to look at the wing on the *other* side. For example, if you were a 3, then you'd also have a 2 wing. Can you see the 2 in your personality? Or if you were a 4, you would also have a 5 wing. Comparing to see whether you have more 2 or 5 in your makeup would help you work out which is your main type.

But more on that later!

We still have important Enneagram concepts to cover.

2.2 OUR ANIMAL DRIVES — THE 27 INSTINCTUAL SUBTYPES

If you've ever used *"It's not my fault — I am wired that way"* to get out of a tricky situation or justify your actions, that was more than just an excuse. You see, there is some *wiring* in all of us. It is in our biological nature to have these instincts, these almost-animal drives that are needed for our survival. They influence our basic personalities, while, paradoxically, our personalities are what enable some of those instincts to affect us more profoundly than others.

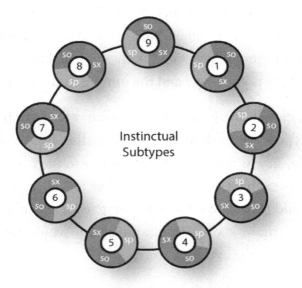

The Instinctual Subtypes

Regardless of which of the 9 types we proudly (or shamefully) own, there are three instincts (also called *subtypes*) per type, that are calling the shots:

1. **Self-preservation (sp)**, which is protecting the self
2. **Social (so)**, which is forming social structures within groups and communities
3. **One-to-one, or sexual (sx)**, which is all about

coupling or the primary sexual relationship such
as marriage

But these instinctual subtypes don't exist in beautiful harmony. Our personality puts the main focus on only one. The other two are just tag-alongs — one existing to support the dominant drive, while the other represents our least developed instinct.

This is also referred to as the *Instinctual Stack*. Think of it as a cupcake. Our least favorite instinct is the liner, the second one is the actual cake, while the dominant one is the most delicious icing on top.

In regards to the main type, one of the three instinctual subtypes can also be considered as a *countertype*. While the two instincts align with the zeal of the type in charge, the third one — the countertype — defies the passion present and goes its own way. It's sort of like the black sheep among a circle of friends. While the other two always seem to agree on things, the black sheep is neither fully accepted, nor does it really understand the gang.

Each person is said to gravitate toward *one* of the instincts, and that influences how your type is expressed. So, for instance, a Type 1 with a one-to-one instinct creates one subtype, while a Type 1 with a self-preservation instinct will be in another subtype, and a Type 1 with a social instinct produces yet another subtype. Whichever subtype

Type 1 leans to the most, all of them share the backbone of the personality in common. They just add different traits to the main personality, creating three instinctual subtypes that manifest basic emotions in unique ways and with different intensities. All three instinctual subtypes may share the same basic Enneatype, however, each of them gives it a unique touch that allows us to have different kinds of, for instance, Ones. Not every One is on the brink of developing OCD, and they don't all live to have the controller in their hands. Those two people may have tested as One on the Enneagram, but they clearly have a different instinctual subtype. Think of the subtypes as different flavors you add to the same meal. Your rice wouldn't be the same if you add turmeric, chili powder, or basil. It will still be rice, yes, but it will surely taste differently.

Since there are three instincts for each Enneagram type, you have probably already guessed that there are 27 instinctual subtypes in total!

They all have different names, which is pretty cool. I mean, are you The Collective Fighter, The Company Woman, or The Movie Star? I think it's quite fun to have a label to play around with, and since there are 27 instinctual subtypes, they get your character *scarily* accurate. When I read the description of my instinctual subtype, I feel both proud and ashamed at once! There are great things about every instinctual subtype, and drawbacks, too.

In Chapter 3, I'm going to reveal to you all 27 different instinctual subtypes, by introducing the three relevant ones for each type. I wonder if you can spot yourself in any of the descriptions! Of course, I've provided you with a really comprehensive quiz to help you type yourself, and it'll help you get your instinctual subtype down, too.

Also, take a look at the image below that shows all the instinctual subtypes.

I can't wait to explore these further with you, as they're one of my favorite parts of the Enneagram.

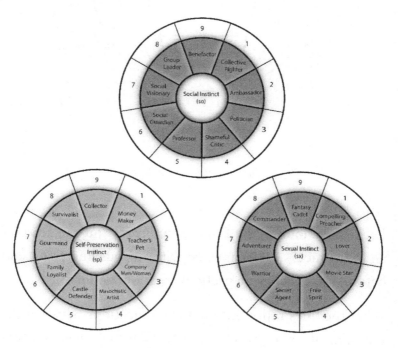

The Instinctual Subtype Names

2.3 WHEN STRESSED AT YOUR WORSE — WHEN GROWING AT YOUR BEST

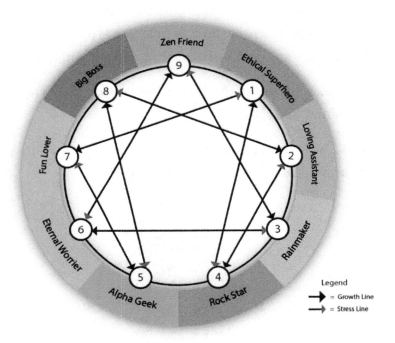

The Growth and Stress Lines

Let's take a look at the Enneagram lines. You can see that all the numbers are connected with various lines. As I said before, this is *not* just a pretty or random pattern.

What the lines represent are the connections between the types, in times of growth and stress. It may seem confusing, but once you get the hang of it, you'll see that it is actually quite simple.

Let's take Type 1 as an example. If you have a look at the arrows, we have a *black arrow* going from Type 1 to Type 7, and we have a *red arrow* going from Type 1 to Type 4.

The black arrow going from a type is called the **Growth Line**. This can also be known as the "direction of integration" or "direction of growth."

So, with a Type 1, its growth line is connected with Type 7.

A growth line represents how you start acting, feeling, and thinking when you're in a good place mentally and emotionally (i.e., you're growing as a person). So this means that when a Type 1 is in a good state, they show the *best* characteristics of Type 7s.

We haven't studied the types yet — we're going to do so in the next section — but I'll quickly describe what this means, so it doesn't seem too abstract. A Type 1 is usually very serious, ordered, and perfectionistic. Type 7s are much more easy-going and love to try tons of new experiences. So when a Type 1 is happy and healthy, they start relaxing more, become more carefree, and are more open to new experiences.

The red arrow going from a type is called the **Stress Line**. This is also known as the "direction of disintegration" or "direction of stress."

So, with a Type 1, its stress line is connected with Type 4.

A stress line represents how you start acting, feeling, and thinking when you're in a *bad* place emotionally. If you're really struggling, whether for a short or long period, you might "travel" along your stress line and pick up the *worst* characteristics of that type. So when a Type 1 is under intense stress, they exhibit the *worst* parts of Type 4s.

Again, I'll describe the types in a ton more detail later, but a Type 1 usually keeps a handle on their emotions and tries to continue on with the task at hand regardless of how they feel. The worst part of Type 4s is that they can fall into deep holes of misery, self-pity, and feeling like a victim at the mercy of everyone else. They push everyone away and sink deeper and deeper. So, in this instance, when a Type 1 is in a really bad way, they show these characteristics of a Type 4.

Understanding growth and stress lines is really important for two reasons:

#1 — So You Can Pick the Right Enneagram Type

It's very, very common to choose the wrong Enneagram type, and quite often, this is down to mistaking your Enneatype for your direction of growth or stress.

For instance, say you are really a Type 1, but you've been going through a really bad time the past few years, it would be really easy to mistype yourself as a Type 4. In the same way, if it's all been smooth sailing lately and you're feeling spontaneous, joyful, and open to new experiences, you could easily mistype yourself as a Type 7.

But when you understand the growth and stress lines, or how you think and act when you are healthy and unhealthy, it is easier to prevent these misidentifications from happening.

#2 — So You Can Understand Yourself Better

It's really important to understand growth and stress lines because they help you to understand those parts of your character that *don't* seem to fit. For example, if a Type 1 was feeling very down, they might say, "I don't feel like myself." Or, perhaps, other people might comment the same — "Oh, she's not herself at the moment." This can make it feel really hard to understand yourself if your character has just totally changed overnight!

But the Enneagram explains it all. These times when we act or feel "out of character" are *not* as unpredictable as we think. I think that can give us comfort and really help us in our path of self-development. Trust me, when it comes to lines of growth and stress, you can get a load of AHA! moments, where you'll say, "Oh, so *that's* why I think that way!"

You'll also, of course, be able to understand when other people act out of character, too!

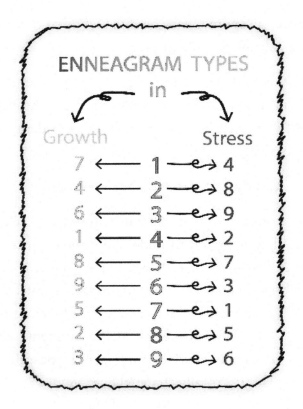

The Growth and Stress Lines Cheatsheet

2.4 GROWING OUT OF YOUR TYPE'S SHELL — THE LEVELS OF DEVELOPMENT

Sometimes we're psychologically healthy, sometimes we're not. And some have a much rougher road than others when it comes to our emotional health. This may be genetic, as mental health issues often pass through families. It may also be environmental. If we've gone through trauma or had an abusive upbringing, that has most likely left us with painful burdens to carry heavily for the rest of our lives. Sadly, this often makes us think and behave in ways that are more destructive to ourselves and others.

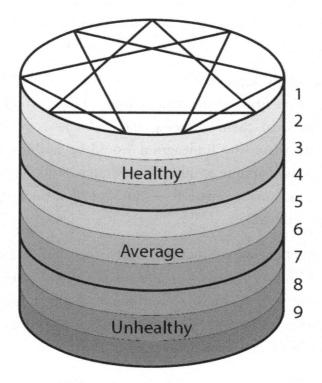

The Levels of Development

But when we start on a path of self-development, we begin to heal and grow. The longer we keep this steady course, the healthier we become. We start to think and behave differently.

To account for this, the Enneagram includes "levels of development." These show how each type thinks and acts at various levels of health. This helps us understand even the darkest events in the human experience, such as suicide and murder. It also gives us insight into various personality disorders and how they can be linked to the Enneagram.

These levels represent the way in which the different parts of an Enneagram type fit into a larger whole. You can think of them as being the *skeleton* of the types. Without them, the Enneagram would be nothing but a straight line of nine points. There would be no dynamism to the personality pattern — no room for their inborn nature to change.

And what are we without the ability to change and grow? Depending on the place in life we are at, we can take a different spot along the continuum of these levels of development. I am not the same *me* when I am stressed as I am when I am satisfied.

The levels of development are quite important, as two people sharing the same type do not necessarily share the same traits at any given point in life — sometimes, one of them will be healthy while the other one is not.

For example, a Type 1 at an exceptionally healthy level of development can be a powerful agent for change, working for humanitarian causes and being truly wise and discerning. On the other hand, a Type 1 in a very unhealthy state can suffer from suicidal tendencies and Obsessive-Compulsive Disorder that rules their lives and tortures their mental health.

It's worth noting that you're not fixed at one level, even at one specific time. For example, it's common for people who have gone through trauma to be "triggered," which can send them on a downward spiral. This might go on for weeks or months, but for some people, it may only be an hour or two. Even though you are usually very healthy, when emotionally challenged you will most likely start showing thoughts and behaviors from some of the most unhealthy levels.

Remember, whatever level you're at, in any timeframe, the Enneagram is *not* here to judge you. It's here to help you. If you find some of your traits or actions listed in the unhealthy levels of development, you might feel angry or scared, or ashamed. But it's okay. Again, I want to remind you about Shadow Work! Shadow Work is all about looking at the parts of ourselves that we really don't want to see. It's always difficult, and it's always painful. It's really awkward and uncomfortable. But if you can sit with that emotion, you *will* come through the other side, and not only that, you'll be wiser, stronger, and more knowledgeable. This, *in itself,* will help you reach higher levels of health.

The key thing when doing Shadow Work is to try to treat yourself with what psychologists call "unconditional positive regard." This means that even though you may not like what you see about yourself, or even hate it, you don't let yourself start hating *you* as a person. You can dislike your behavior, thoughts, or traits, without condemning or punishing yourself.

If you end up struggling with this, remembering these three things may help:

1. The Enneagram is a tool for *understanding,* not for *judging.*
2. Whatever difficult traits you have, you also have some amazing ones.
3. There is always room for growth.

The levels of development are grouped as follows:

- **Healthy** — levels 1 through 3 are levels of self-freedom; you let go of your ego and you are in control of yourself. You are aware of your true self, your personality, your underlying emotions, and your driving force, and you are at peace with it.
- **Average** — levels 4 through 6 are levels focused on self-image; you want others to see you in a certain way. Therefore you use social roles,

manipulation, and controlling others to reinforce your identity.

- **Unhealthy** — levels 7 through 9 are self-destructive levels; you are stuck in a vicious circle of subconscious habitual destructive patterns. Your behavior is driven by the core fear of your Enneagram type.

2.5 GUT, HEAD, HEART — THE THREE CENTERS OF THE ENNEAGRAM

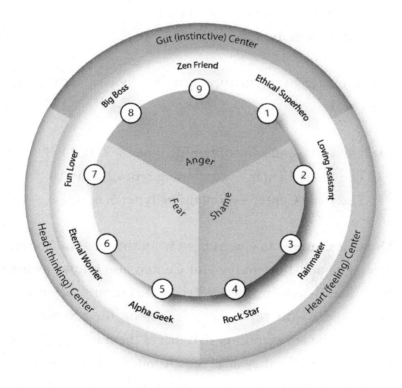

The Centers

The final thing we'll be looking at is Centers, which are also known as "Triads." Think of the structure of the Enneagram as a 3 by 3 arrangement — a whole that has three Centers, each of which holds three Enneagram types.

The Centers explain two things:

1. Which unhealthy emotion we fixate on
2. How we experience reality — through our gut (sensing/instinctual), our head (thinking/intellectual), or through our heart (feeling/emotional)

The Enneagram's structure can be divided into three equal parts:

1. The Gut Center — containing types 8, 9, and 1
2. The Heart Center — containing types 2, 3, and 4
3. The Head Center — containing types 5, 6, and 7

The Gut Center: As you can see from the diagram above, types 8, 9, and 1 are in the Gut Center, also known as the Body, Sensing, or Instinctive Triad. This means they experience the world through their gut or their senses or instinct. The core emotion that drives them is *anger*. Ones internalize it — they are mostly angry at themselves, Eights externalize it — they are mostly angry with the outer world, and Nines forget the anger — they pile up these angry feelings inside so they remain calm. The types in the Gut Center express themselves directly and with honesty.

The Heart Center: Types 2, 3, and 4 are in the Heart Center, also known as the Shame, Feeling, or Emotional Triad. They experience reality through their emotions, and usually make decisions based on how they feel. Twos are focused on the emotions of the others, Threes have trouble recognizing and connecting with their (and other people's) feelings, and Fours are mainly concerned with how they feel inside. The core emotion of these three types is *shame* and feeling they're worthless and not good enough. This can really undermine their confidence and make them behave in destructive ways.

The Head Center: Types 5, 6, and 7 are in the Head Center, also known as the Intellectual, Thinking, or Fear Triad. They experience reality through thinking and spend a lot of time mentally processing. They have problems with feeling *fear and anxiety*, and this can really hold them back. Fives embrace these emotions, Sixes are completely out of touch with their fear, and Sevens avoid the feelings and distract themselves so as not to get in touch with these sensations inside.

We'll look at each type and their placement in the Centers in the coming pages.

A BRIEF ENNEAGRAM SUMMARY

MAIN TAKEAWAY POINTS

The Enneagram is a dynamic system in which the various patterns of how different people think, feel, and act, are described. It is not a crystal ball, but discovering your path will certainly feel like looking into one. You will finally become aware of your true self and see the way in which you've been interpreting the outer world and managing your emotions.

Here are the most important takeaway points about this powerful self-improving system that you need to know of:

- The Enneagram basically means *Ennea = 9* and *gram = diagram.*
- It is a diagram, a map that shows 9 main personality types and how they are connected with each other.
- Each of the nine types has different personality

traits and their own pattern of thinking and acting.

- The Enneagram is a personal growth system that explains *why* we feel, think, and behave a certain way. It shows us our underlying emotions and driving force, which allows us to finally understand and get to know ourselves.

- You can be only one Enneagram type, which is formed before you come into this world.

- The Enneagram shows you more than just your main type and its basic personality traits. It sheds light on all the aspects of your character — the good and bad, the strengths and weaknesses. It shows you your main motivation, as well as your blind spot.

- The system is composed of the main types, wings, instinctual subtypes, growth and stress lines, levels of development, and centers.

- The Enneagram is composed of three centers: Gut (types 8, 9, 1), Heart (types 2, 3, 4), and Head (types 5, 6, 7).

- Each type has three subtypes: Self-Preservation (sp), Social (so), and Sexual (sx).

- Each type has two adjacent wings, and in most cases, one of these wings is dominant, although the wings can be balanced. The wings are the personality traits of your neighbor types that influence the way that *you* think and act.

- Each type has its own growth and stress lines, which means that they take on traits of another type, depending on whether they are healthy or not.

- The Enneagram is not a system that will allow you to *change* who you are, but to *accept* all of the parts of your personality, so you can *grow* and be happier.

- If you calculate all of the possible personality variations with the main types, instinctual subtypes wings, and lines of health, you are looking at 486 different personality combinations.

- You can share many traits with other types (remember, there are 486 versions, after all), but your main type (1–9) will always stay the same.

- The wisdom of this whole system is to find the thing that motivates *you*. The key to self-development is to learn why you are doing the things you are doing, and what is the primary motivation that shapes your whole being. Only by understanding your type and all of its components can you discover your true self.

- It is your motivation that powers your existence — don't obsess over these personality traits or combos, but ask yourself *WHY DO I DO THE THINGS I DO?* Once you figure out what your driving force is, everything will make much more sense.

CHAPTER 3 - NAKED WITH THE ENNEAGRAM

E very living person can live a happy and fulfilling life and even reach greatness. The main obstacle that prevents us from doing so is not our inability to tap into that potential, or even see what we are capable of, but the fact that we genuinely believe that we know ourselves. We have been adding so many layers and layers of personalities, character traits, and coping mechanisms to the *real me* inside, that we have come to believe that's who we actually are.

Ever since we were born, we have been living our life in a sort of automatic, almost mechanical way. We go about our lives without actually putting in some conscious effort — we just accept that things have to be done in this pre-determined way. But who determined that for us? Our parents, caregivers, teachers, and general society from our early stages in life! We then started, one by one, to put all of these different coatings on so that the *real me* is barely even recognizable now. Like putting makeup on, we have been beautifying our imperfections all this time.

But, without us really knowing the *one* we started this life with in the first place, we will stay forever lost.

Try to see it this way. Let's say that you suffered abuse of some kind as a child. That clearly makes you a victim, but perhaps the last thing you want is to be one. So you put on a mask of strength and independence. You live your life not quite fitting and compensate for that with all of these layers of your ego that turn you into a more distant, self-righteous elitist, or perhaps an arrogant being. Do you honestly believe that you can be truly satisfied with yourself with all of these fake structures of your personality? Unless you learn how to peel those layers back so that you can get to the wounded you inside, you will never be able to act accordingly and make healthy choices.

Your Enneagram type is here to help you do that. Of course, your situation may not be as extreme as the example above, but you get my meaning. Waking up from your automatic acting is the only way you can form healthy relationships, find the right career path, and learn how to fully breathe life in.

It almost feels a little bit naked — showing the real you to the rest of the world can be scary. But that is who you are! Why should you be stuck in a comfortable maze just because you are scared that the straight road to your happiness can be bumpy?

Think of knowing your Enneagram type as peeling off layers of your being. One by one, you will get rid of the things you have been putting there for a really long time until finally, you expose the core. You see yourself truly and find out that, even after all this time, you are still the same person. You understand why things happen to you, and most importantly, what you can do to make them right.

Ready to show a little piece of your soul? Let's explore human nature together!

Type 1

The Ethical Superhero

At their BEST:

organized
rational
honest
ethical
reliable
productive
idealistic

At their WORST:

critical
inflexible
controlling
anxious
frustrated
impatient
dissatisfied

Shareable Quote:

You may think I don't kiss or hug enough,
but on the inside — I burst with love.
My urge to control and correct sometimes may annoy,
but it's how I keep you safe — not something I enjoy.
I may overreact and have everything in an orderly display,
but stick with me, and even an apocalypse we can slay.

3.1 TYPE 1

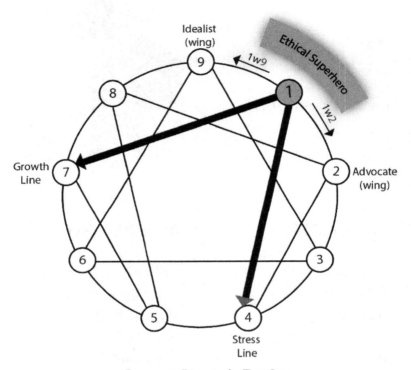

Enneagram Diagram for Type One

Name: Type 1 — The Ethical Superhero

AKA: The Idealist, The Judge, The Critic, The Reformer, The Perfectionist

Personality: If you are a Type 1, you strive to be good and do the right thing, so you can stay on the responsible track and never be blamed for lack of quality or correction. You are the *parental voice* among your circle of friends — not necessarily patronizing, but always doing your best to instill order.

Although, in all fairness, you can sometimes sound like *the mom* — forcing your friend to put on a sweater when the temperature drops lower, convincing them of the severity of the consequences.

You are highly ethical, with powerful views about morality — you have a black and white view of what is right and what is wrong. You have a strong sense of duty and want to improve the world in some way. You have very high standards and are very serious about them, so when you and others fall short of your expectations, you can be very critical.

You hold back many emotions, but sometimes, resentment and anger can simmer under the surface.

At your best, you're a capable, well-organized, and powerful agent for change. You can be truly heroic and go down in history for your noble deeds. At your worst, you can be too controlling, addicted to being better.

You can sometimes contradict yourself and get in your own way by overdoing or overcontrolling, which can take a toll on your self-confidence and result in judgy emotions. However, once you learn to put your inner critic on a leash, your reliable and idealism-focused nature can amount to excellence.

Your Worst Fear: Type 1 fears mess. They are afraid of imperfections and of being perceived as someone who does not meet expectations, someone who has to be corrected. Any form of imbalance makes them lose their grip.

If you are a One, that might mean fighting with your partner for not putting the toilet seat down, or not returning the mayo to the right spot in the fridge, next to the ketchup.

Your Heart's Desire: To live in a world where everything makes sense. For a One, that can even mean having the cups in the cupboard arranged in a specific order (demitasse to large, duh!). Ones crave order, balance, and perfection, so they are always on the quest of fixing, improving, and meeting self-appointed high standards before they can relax and enjoy life.

Your Biggest Sin: Being control freaks. You'll know you have a hardcore Type 1 on a vacation when you're visiting lavender fields or attending a cooking class instead of jumping in the ocean with your clothes on.

Wings:

1w9 The Idealist — Your trait is optimism, and you strive to be morally good. You make calm and rational choices, mostly from a detached, objective standpoint. You care for your community and are constantly defending or upholding values. The weak thing about you is the stubbornness that takes over when someone challenges you.

1w2 The Advocate — You are a true activist at heart. You are always looking to volunteer or help those in need, trying to make a real difference. You are passionate, principled, and crave social change and more justice in the world. You have an ability to improve, and more often than not, you tend to sacrifice your needs for the greater good. Your main weakness is that you can get quite obsessive and frustrated.

Subtypes:

Self-preservation Type 1 — The Money Maker

You create security through money and material achievements. The home, family, food, and savings are of great concern to you. You want to overcome nature and impose order on the material world to make sure you're turning chaos into order.

Usually, self-preservation Ones have chaotic family backgrounds — ones where they were in charge of providing, even from a young age.

Stability is your primary goal, and you feel the urge to always have everything planned out, with the compulsion of holding all the strings yourself. That is why you are constantly in a highly alert state — ready to act the second something deviates from your plan.

Social Type 1 — The Collective Fighter

You hold a secure social role and follow the expectations of this role. When you're in your own sphere, you're generous and friendly. Outside your comfort zone, the chaos of people doing things the "wrong way" gets your back up.

Socially, you are not that adaptable. You have a strong need to teach others the correct way by showing examples. You are almost like a philosophy professor — too intellectual to understand, always making others feel inferior in your presence.

Sexual Type 1 — The Compelling Preacher (the countertype)

The sexual Ones are focused on fixing others, and unlike the other two subtypes, not that focused on perfectionism. You are angrier, more impatient, and super compelling, which is what sets you apart from the other two instincts and makes you the countertype.

You have a very strict code on what is good behavior and what isn't. You keep yourself firmly under control and if you break one of your own rules, you beat yourself up about it. You are very concerned about keeping your partner's attention, but you may feel jealous of their freedom while criticizing them for it.

Stress Number: 4. When stress swoops in, Ones tend to show the unhealthy side that is usual for Type 4s. The self-critic claims its territory, and they soon begin to face trouble functioning. They become moody, indignant, deeply irrational, and even take on self-hating feelings. This self-destructiveness, if left unattended to, can lead to depression.

Growth Number: 7. Once feelings of security take over, and the core emotion — anger — subsides, Ones take on the traits of the Sevens. They find it easier to relax, can make spontaneous and not pre-determined choices, and overall, they become really fun to be around. The calmness of their mind shushes their inner critic and allows them to see that there is a beautiful side to imperfections as well.

Center: Positioned in the top right corner of the Enneagram circumference, Ones belong in the instinctive or the Gut Center. Your core emotion is anger, but you also put a huge portion of your focus on judgment and the achievement of standards. You crave structure, control, and order, which keeps you energetically attentive. To make a decision, you go to your gut and trust your instincts. You embrace your center and internalize your anger.

Famous 1s: Plato, Confucius, Joan of Arc, Gandhi, Nelson Mandela, Hermione Granger (*Harry Potter*), Osama bin Laden, Martha Stewart, Kate Middleton, Meryl Streep, Celine Dion, Michelle Obama, Batman, Jerry Seinfeld, John Paul II.

Shareable Quote: *You may think I don't kiss or hug enough, but on the inside — I burst with love. My urge to control and correct sometimes may annoy, but it's how I keep you safe — not something I enjoy. I may overreact and have everything in an orderly display, but stick with me, and even an apocalypse we can slay.*

MY INNER WORLD

What I Like About Being this Type: I enjoy working to make the world a better place and holding firm to my ethics and standards. I appreciate my own self-discipline, dedication, and responsibility, and I enjoy the way my mind works — I use logic and wisdom to put the facts together and make good decisions.

What's Hard About Being this Type: Sometimes, the responsibility feels too much, and I feel like I can't match up to the ideal. It's hard being disappointed with myself and others, especially when others don't try hard enough or take things seriously. I struggle with feeling angry and anxious, and sometimes it's very hard for me to relax.

Your Personal Vices (addictions): You're extremely disciplined and self-controlled and concerned with doing what is right, so it's highly unlikely you'd get addicted to illegal drugs. It's more likely you'd get obsessive about exercise, vitamins, and diets. You might control your eating to the point that you don't eat enough, or suffer from anorexia or bulimia. Since you carry a lot of tension, you may end up relying on alcohol to relax you, which can lead to addiction.

Typical Thinking Patterns: Your mind goes to what is wrong, and what can be improved. You see this in a clear, logical way, and your thoughts are ordered and methodical. You clearly see details, and immediately evaluate them. When you interact with others, your thought patterns will often be on evaluating them in terms of their morality.

Typical Feeling Patterns: When you see something that can be improved on, it both agitates and inspires you at once, moving you to action. When you're in the process of righting wrongs, you feel strong and capable. But frustration about your own imperfections or those of others leads to anger and can drag you down into hopelessness, too.

SELF-DEVELOPMENT

When You're Very Healthy (levels 1 to 3): You can become very wise. You have a strong sense of right and wrong, and can be very discerning in seeing what is good and what needs to be changed. You're brave and self-sacrificing, without even thinking about it — you're just doing what needs to be done.

When You're Very Unhealthy (levels 7 to 9): It feels like you're being tortured by people doing the wrong things all around you. This can make you a hypocrite because in condemning, judging, and punishing them, you become just as bad as them. You can get very depressed or even have a breakdown, as it feels like you've got the weight of the world on your shoulders, being the only good person fighting against a sea of evil and wrong.

When You're Somewhere in Between (levels 4 to 6): You're critical of yourself and others, and have extremely high standards that motivate you, but also frustrate you. You are emotionally detached, not letting any of your emotions overwhelm you, and are judgmental of those who do. You're a workaholic, and very well-organized and fastidious.

How to Maximize Your Potential: Mindfulness can be exceptionally helpful, because it gives you a break from constantly evaluating and judging. With mindfulness, the idea is to notice and pay attention to things, without immediately forming an opinion on them. You're a great observer already — now use that observer mindset.

Red Flags to Watch Out for: If you're a Type 1, watch out for the tendency to always focus on what's wrong with things. Not only does this hold you back from finding the solutions you crave, but you also overlook achievements and may forget to celebrate them. Other red flags include tension, rigidity, and an obsession with correcting things.

Self-Development Activities: Given their perfection-oriented, ideal-seeking, somewhat-controlling, and criticizing nature, Ones go about their days carrying a lot of weight on their shoulders. The mind of a One is on overload more often than not. Just think of it as a pressure cooker — not the modern electric ones, but those from the 50s. Be one second too late, and kaboom! Chicken pieces exploding all over the kitchen.

Just like with a pressure cooker, Ones need to find the right way to release the steam so that mind explosions don't happen. They need healthy activities in which they can shake off their high-strung attitude and OCD tendencies so they can focus on their best traits. Because guess what? Ones can be true darlings when they're not pulled back by the weight of the world.

Finding the Balance — Ones have a somewhat dualistic nature — they always think of themselves as not nearly ideal, while doing their best to have others perceive them as perfect. Somewhere along the way between harsh self-criticism and pushing to reach the highest bar, dissatisfaction swoops in. If this sounds familiar, focus on finding the balance. Do your best to get stuff done, but once things start to get *just a bit too much,* pause and say to yourself, "I am doing my best." Give yourself a pat on the back for trying, even if you cannot get the job done. Remember, no one can win them all!

Channeling the Anger — Remember how we said that Ones are not fans of showing emotions, but that anger and discontent can simmer under the surface? To prevent these feelings from boiling over and spilling onto whoever's holding the other end of the stick, you need to find a way to channel your anger. Repressed emotions can be quite destructive; maybe you have heard the Buddha quote, "Holding onto anger is like drinking poison and expecting the other person to die." What I'm trying to say is, instead of taking it out on your partner for buying peaches instead of nectarines (yes, there IS a difference!), go and punch a pillow. Then come back and explain in a calm way.

Morning jogs, hitting the gym every afternoon, or taking a martial-art class can be a healthy way to channel these emotions.

Forcing Yourself to Relax — Ones have a hard time laying back and relaxing because of their constant whirlwind of obligations and unfinished chores. It can be tricky, but try to fit *relaxation time* into your schedule (yes, actually write it down in that planner of yours!). It can be as simple as a half-hour bubble bath or a short walk on the beach. Something that can just let you loosen up a bit each day.

Shushing the Inner Critic — Whenever you hear that loud voice inside screaming at you for not doing everything up to par, just smile and say, "I hear you." Self-criticism is beneficial in small doses but destructive in heaps. Make sure to remind yourself that you are doing the best you can, and move on. Doing this regularly can help you change that outlook.

Other things that can help you transform your behavior and lead to self-development include:

- Cutting back on the To-Do lists and making plans only for the most important things.
- Finding a hobby that you are not particularly good at, but do it for the pure joy it brings — yes, dancing with two left feet can be super fun!
- Trying yoga and/or meditation — these practices will not only help you tame anger, but they will also help you reduce stress and relax.

Doing Your Best in Relationships — Although revealing your soul and showing emotions is not something that comes naturally to you, Ones can be the partner or friend for life everyone is looking for. You may not blurt out *I love you's* every five seconds, but you will do your best to show how you feel. You are responsible, committed, reliable, and you will make anyone feel safe and sound in your presence.

However, your need to head towards perfection can sometimes be an issue. If you're a One, make sure to:

- Cut back on re-doing things. Yes, your partner

may have put the pasta where the rice should go when unloading the groceries, but rethink your urge to move it. Appreciate the gesture instead.

- Tell others how much you appreciate the things they're doing, even though you would have done them slightly differently.
- Ask a friend to let you know when your attitude gets too criticizing, so you will know what you should work on changing.
- Learn to apologize. When you notice your attitude has gone a bit too far, go back and apologize for your actions. You may be a hotshot One, but you will need the other person to know that you also realize that things went too far.
- Readjust your tone when you notice yourself getting too harsh.

Thriving at Work — Thanks to their perfection-directed goals, Ones can be the real hardworking bees at the office. However, this can also be treated as a fault. For a One to thrive at work, they need to follow three simple rules:

1. Appreciate the achievements: stop dwelling on the past mistakes
2. Get over imperfections: sometimes the deadlines are so tight that the only positive outcome is to have the job done — even with flaws
3. Do not take more than you can chew on: It is okay

to admit that you cannot finish something and
pass the work to another coworker

Jobs and Career Paths: If you want someone reliable that will do the job thoroughly, in an organized manner, and without missing a detail, then hire a One. Ones need a well-structured working environment where they know what is expected of them. They need to have rules to follow and a specific goal to meet. Ones will never argue if you take a bite of their paycheck for making a mistake.

Given their controlling personality, urge to instill order/discipline/knowledge, and high standards, the best career paths for Type 1s include working as police officers, judges, activists, detectives, or social workers. On the other hand, the jobs that a Type 1 should, perhaps, steer clear from, are:

Administrative Assistants — Since Ones are deadly afraid of making mistakes and not being right, it will be hard to complete tons of different tasks at the same time and not make an error. This will leave Ones feeling miserable and not satisfied with their job.

Retail Representatives — If a One doesn't see a purposeful and immediate result of the things they're doing, they can sometimes become inflexible and dogmatic, which is never a good thing if you're working as a retail representative. And given the inconsistent working hours, this can throw a One off-balance and make them hate their job.

Activities and Hobbies: Thanks to their high standards and a strong focus on morality, the hobbies that Ones will deeply enjoy include volunteering, tutoring, and fundraising.

SPIRITUALITY

Spiritual Struggles: Remember the stress line that brings out the negative traits of Type 4? As a Type 1, you may have noticed that challenging times require great strength from you — the strength to overcome the most negative ideas about yourself. These ideas couldn't be further from the spiritual truth of who you are.

So, part of your struggle may be coming to see such negative ideas for what they are, and coming to a greater understanding of your true self and spiritual nature. You may also struggle to connect with others on a deeper level, as your ongoing resentment simmers under the surface. Once again, learning to relax can help to ease this tension and with time, free up more energy to experience a broader range of experiences in life — beyond your overall mission.

Your Life Lesson and the Path of Integration: Less thinking and doing, more being. Remember, when you're doing well, you take on the positive traits of Type 7, which is all about being and enjoying the present moment. You will eventually be able to experience true joy, able to let go of the burden of responsibility.

When you practice this, you can eventually operate at your peak. This means you will still be able to fulfill your spiritual mission but in a much calmer and more balanced way. You will be able to achieve your spiritual purpose without doing so at the expense of your own joy and happiness. Accepting the present moment and yourself is a practice that will accelerate the process.

Some of the important spiritual areas to focus on are acceptance, the forgiveness of self and others, and developing a knowledge of your inherent worthiness, without conditions. Non-judgmental awareness will help you to observe without reacting in the agitated way that you usually might when you're exposed to triggers.

Daily Affirmations and Transformations for Type Ones:

- I NOW LET GO of my need to do everything myself
- I NOW ACCEPT the help that others offer
- I NOW LET GO of the high bar I have appointed myself
- I NOW ACCEPT that the things I do are enough
- I NOW LET GO of my urge to correct other people's actions

- I NOW ACCEPT that we are different and that cannot be changed
- I NOW LET GO of trying to hold all of the strings
- I NOW ACCEPT that sometimes I will make a mistake
- I NOW LET GO of looking for the faults in everything
- I NOW ACCEPT and appreciate good deeds, no matter how flawed

COMPATIBILITY — HOW WELL "ONE" SUITS THE OTHER TYPES

Type 1: Seeing two Ones in a relationship is like watching two contestants fighting for the same prize — criticizing the other one with the goal of reaching perfectionism. They have respect for each other, which is undeniable, but they can both be quite the hotshots at times.

Type 2: They often come together with shared values and complement each other well. However, the problem here is that they cannot express their needs clearly, so they both risk feeling a bit left out.

Type 3: Both idealists, together they can achieve greatness. However, Threes may become stifled by a One's rigidity and criticism of their methods.

Type 4: Fours bring the expression and spontaneity that Ones overlook, helping to bring balance. They complement each other well on that level, but their different ways of dealing with problems may pose an issue.

Type 5: They have a common interest in intellectual stimulation, which can work out very well. Fives are more flexible in their outlook, which can lead to conflict.

Type 6: Sixes and Ones have a lot in common in their approach to life, so they make a good combination. They also develop a strong foundation of loyalty in their relationship. A Six is warmer and finds it easier to connect with others, which can help tame the social awkwardness that Ones can sometimes face.

Type 7: As opposites, Ones and Sevens bring balance to each other. Since Seven is the growth line for Ones, imagine how well they would go together when the One is at their best? Sevens help to lighten things up, which contrasts the heaviness that a Type One can fall into at times.

Type 8: They both are concerned with battling injustice and have that superhero personality at times, however, their different approach to morality can be an issue.

Type 9: Nines and Ones can go well together because Nines are more interested in harmony and don't feel the need to prove a point or engage in conflict. Nines are easier to get along with, so while they share many ideals with Type Ones, this allows for a smoother path.

MISIDENTIFICATION

It is common for Ones to misidentify themselves as Fives, since they both correspond to the same thinking type of Carl Jung — One in an extroverted way, while Five is the introverted one.

However, once you look more deeply, you will see that Ones and Fives have different standards — Ones always judging from their idealistic standpoint, Fives focused on investigating and wondering about the nature of principles. Ones being moralists, Fives being inventors.

AN OUTSIDER'S GUIDE TO TYPE 1S

To get along with me, you need to understand my values and why they are important to me. Even if you don't agree, it is essential that you acknowledge where I'm coming from. You might think that I'm being cold, insensitive, or uncaring, but I'm not intentionally trying to be hurtful — I just don't give emotions or sentiment as much importance as other people do. Logic and reason is the way I operate.

If you try to make me do something that conflicts with my morals, integrity or just the way I have decided I do things, don't expect me to conform. I respect honesty, and if you try to lie to me we will have a problem.

. Since it's difficult for me to relax, I enjoy the company of people that make it easy to enjoy myself, as long as they don't expect me to go completely wild.

If we need to resolve conflict, I prefer not to bring emotion into it. I prefer to work through things rationally, keeping to relevant protocols and principles. It's easy for me to ignore the context of a conflict, as I stick to my personal rules as much as possible. I might need someone to explain the bigger picture if there's any chance of me being more flexible than I would be otherwise.

Type 2

The Loving Assistant

At their BEST:

loving
generous
empathic
helpful
caring
sociable
thoughtful

At their WORST:

possessive
needy
manipulative
emotional
martyrlike
low self-esteem
aggressive

Shareable Quote:

I give you all my love and care;
just say the word, and I'll be there.
When you need my help, it makes my day,
"What would I do without you?" is what I want to hear you say.
I am warm and kind,
I've got a lot to give;
I hope that all my mistakes you can forgive.

3.2 TYPE 2

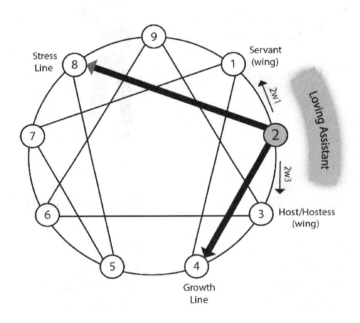

Enneagram Diagram for Type Two

Name: Type 2 — The Loving Assistant

AKA: The Martyr, The Caregiver, The Lover, The Pleaser, The Helper

Personality: When I think of a Two, the first thing that pops to mind is that old Cheap Trick song: "I want you to want me, I need you to need me, I'd love you to love me, I'm begging you to beg me." Because that is exactly what

Two wants — *they want to be wanted.* The idea of having someone that needs them in their life is what powers Two's existence.

This may make them sound like a naïve bunch without a shred of self-worth, but if you don't have a Two in your life, I suggest you go out and get one. Okay, okay, *Can you do a quick Enneagram test for me?* is not exactly how you should start a conversation, but don't worry, you can sense a Two from miles away thanks to the warmth that oozes out of their pores.

One of my closest friends is a Two, and I don't know if I would have been able to go through the toughest periods of my life without her by my side. Pay Emma a visit during a crisis, and it will feel like a free therapy session — only less judgmental. If you feel like crying, a Kleenex box is always at your fingertips. If you want to eat your feelings away, a bowl of ice cream is on its way. It's almost like she has supernatural gifts — always knowing just what others need, even before they realize it themselves.

If you are a Type 2, you're warm-hearted, friendly, generous, and giving. You sacrifice yourself for others, and this can be a great strength, or sometimes a terrible weakness. You can be pleasing people to your own detriment — taking care of the needs of everyone else while forgetting about your own. Sometimes you do things for others that people don't ask for, and then feel resentful that you're not loved and cared for in the same way.

At your best, you're a powerful force of warmth and love, and can totally change people's lives. You're the parent everyone wished they had, and you nurture people around you and heal broken hearts. At your worst, you get super insecure and cannot function without relying on someone else. Your need to have someone that appreciates and accepts you may push you into forming unhealthy relationships just for the sake of having any kind of companionship.

Your Worst Fear: That you're unwanted and unloved. The idea of being cast aside by people who have taken a huge chunk of your heart sends chills down your spine.

Your Heart's Desire: To feel loved, cherished, and cared for. The thing that Twos want most is for others to admit how much they appreciate having them in their life. Which is why they are so invested in giving and caring — realizing that you cherish their love and effort is a drug they're addicted to.

Your Biggest Sin: Being manipulative — Twos "give to get" but make it seem like they need nothing in return. Their care and affection can sometimes be pre-calculated. They hide under a "martyr" mask and can sneak up on your guilt, manipulating you only so they can scratch their emotional itch.

Wings:

2w1 The Servant — You sacrifice yourself in service for high ideals. A 2w1 is the first one to offer their help when you're in crisis and the last one you will see complaining about completing tasks that others avoid. You are generous, warm, and kind. The 1w is the pillar of your personality — giving you an empowering pull once your serving urge pushes you a bit too far. The weakness arises when the empowering One tugs the leash a bit too strongly — stressed 2w1s aim for the perfection of Type 1s, and become self-judging.

2w3 The Host or Hostess — You want to take care of others in a way that makes other people look up to you with admiration. 2w3s host parties that everyone wants to attend. You are more social than those with 1w, and your charismatic nature is hard to resist. You don't need an ice breaker with 2w3 — they are chatty enough to make everyone feel pleasant in their presence. The bad part about this Two and 3w combo is that their pride can get overinflated. Two always doing their best to please, and 3w worrying about how their actions are perceived. They are too sensitive to criticism, struggling to grasp self-awareness.

Subtypes:

Self-preservation Type 2 — The Teacher's Pet (the countertype)

You get the attention and affection you crave by unconsciously seducing everybody in a child-like manner. Self-preservation Twos aim for cuteness and always look kind of youngish. You are almost like a wounded cuddly animal — it is impossible not to love you, which makes you feel privileged. SP Twos are the definition of a teacher's pet — too charming to be anything less than a favorite.

Just like with the other Twos, this subtype is also focused on pleasing others as a way to get some love in return, but SP Twos are far more reserved. You like being around people, but the possibility of getting rejected scares you to death. Your conflicting push-and-pull nature makes you the countertype of Two.

Self-preservation Twos avoid getting in touch with themselves, which pushes them on a self-indulgent path. They detach from their inner-deprivation by seeking instant pleasers for their sensations in the form of shopping, partying, or drinking.

Social Type 2 — The Ambassador

You aim for social approval and can easily read people. You tune in to other people's needs and wants, and this helps you create a central position in a community or organization. They can't do without you, as you're the glue that holds everything together. You don't usually seek the limelight, though.

You feel satisfied once you've conquered the audience, and you seduce the environment by spreading influence. Compared to the other two subtypes, the Ambassador is usually the more *powerful* Two — one that is exceptionally successful in their line of work or owns their own company.

The Social Two is ambitious to climb to the top and probably has been pleasing important people for a long time — think "being friends with your teacher" kind of long.

Sexual Type 2 — The Lover

You gain attention, deep connection, rapport, and admiration from people on a one-on-one level. You're seductive, drawing people in, maybe in a sexual way, maybe not. You can hypnotize people with your body language and your aura of care. The Sexual Two is the type of person that always gets what they want without even asking for it. All they have to do is bring their seduction to the mix, and they can rule the world.

When their needs are not met, this type can manifest more aggressively, demanding recognition, respect, and attention. They justify their somewhat invasive actions by hiding behind the name of love — everything they ever wanted was to be loved.

While the other subtypes are often misidentified with other Enneatypes, the sexual instinct has inherited most of the Two's traits.

Stress Number: 8. When you're under stress and not feeling good, you can become domineering and aggressive. If people don't meet your emotional needs when you are kind and giving, you feel like you have to spell it out in a forceful way to demand what you want. Reaching to Eight, Two can become more confident to take the wheel in their own hands and lead the direction for once. The strengths of Eight help Twos be bolder and unafraid to take some risks.

This self-assurance will allow Twos to interact with others more freely, and if they see their sudden ability to enter conflicts as a positive thing, Twos can actually step away from the emotional tangles they have with other people.

Growth Number: 4. When you're in a good place, you start to reclaim your needs, just like a Four would do. You nurture yourself and realize that self-care is important. Instead of running to other people to get your emotional needs in check, you find a way to access your feelings in a way that balances out your urge to focus on others and gives you more confidence to say what *you* want for a change.

By turning to Four for help, Twos can strengthen their connection to self, and finally realize that treating themselves can actually support the relationships in their life, rather than threaten them.

Center: You're in the Heart, Emotional, or Feeling Center. This means you have problems with toxic shame — that is the go-to emotion that can hold you back. You can sometimes feel like you're not good enough and don't deserve love or respect. Twos avoid their center and externalize their feelings — they are more concerned with others than themselves.

Famous 2s: Mother Teresa, Luciano Pavarotti, Lionel Richie, Stevie Wonder, Priscilla Presley, Elizabeth Taylor, Martin Sheen, Princess Diana, Brigitte Bardot, Monica Lewinsky, Peeta Mell (*The Hunger Games*).

Shareable Quote: *I give you all my love and care; just say the word, and I'll be there. When you need my help, it makes my day, "What would I do without you?" is what I want to hear you say. I am warm and kind, I've got a lot to give; I hope that all my mistakes you can forgive.*

MY INNER WORLD

What I Like About Being this Type: I love being someone that others can count on. It makes me happy to be able to help and support other people when they need it. I'm very caring by nature, so it's rewarding when I can use this to make a difference in others' lives.

What's Hard About Being this Type: It's difficult when others don't reciprocate my generosity, which makes me feel unappreciated. This sometimes makes me resent these people and feel bitter. I want others to feel guilty for not giving back to me and making me feel unwanted. It can be frustrating having these expectations of others, and I can get manipulative at times.

Your Personal Vices (addictions): Anything that can elicit attention and sympathy from others. For example, hypochondria. You may compensate for your unmet emotional needs by overeating or indulging in other substances in an attempt to fill the void.

Typical Thinking Patterns: They're always on the lookout for ways to help others. This could be anything from small gestures to situations where they can have a greater impact. If they start to feel that someone is not meeting their expectations, preventing their own needs from being met, they might start looking for ways to force reciprocation from others. This could be through guilt-tripping others or manipulating situations.

Typical Feeling Patterns: De-emphasizing their own feelings and prioritizing others'. This can lead to a lot of denial about what their true feelings are. Behind the resentment, there are feelings of hurt or abandonment from not having their needs met. They feel their best when they are operating healthily, giving to others without doing so to their own detriment. This allows them to feel emotionally fulfilled and useful.

SELF-DEVELOPMENT

When You're Very Healthy (levels 1 to 3): You are a true angel in the lives of others. You feel it's a privilege that other people let you into their hearts, and you tread carefully, giving them unconditional love and not overstepping boundaries. You are also kind and loving to yourself and feel much calmer.

When You're Very Unhealthy (levels 7 to 9): When in a bad place, you feel victimized and abused by other people, and this gives you an excuse to behave badly. You feel bitter and angry inside because all you do is give, give, give, so it is pretty disappointing when you don't get what you think you deserve in return. But even then, you do not want to become a burden to others or be perceived as anything less than a good person. To avoid falling apart or entering darker corners, you end up indulging in food pleasures or using alcohol or drugs to numb the dissatisfaction.

When You're Somewhere in Between (levels 4 to 6): This is where people-pleasing creeps in. The issue with focusing on the needs of others is that it's not genuine.

You don't do this so the people around you will feel better. You do it so *you* can feel better by thinking you've made others happy. This comes from insecurity and the fear that you won't be seen as the true helper you are when you function at your healthiest level. Trying to make others like you has a negative effect on your self-esteem. Instead of being happy with what you do, you constantly tell yourself that you're not enough. Your fixation on other people's needs leads to suppressing your true personality. How can others see the real you when you never make a real connection?

Codependency and possessiveness can also develop at this level. You may become overly self-sacrificial and expect others to reciprocate in the same way. You can become worn out and begin to neglect your own needs. Others may find you intrusive in your quest to be seen as someone that can offer them help in some way. You may also engage in destructive behavior in an attempt to have your needs met.

How to Maximize Your Potential: It's all about balance. You can only give so much without becoming depleted. You can give your best to others when you are already fulfilled within yourself. If you have no energy left from helping others too much, what is there to give? It is almost like having a pan simmering over high heat. If you don't pour enough liquid in, the food will burn. The same goes for a not-so-healthy Two. If you just give and give, without pouring some of that love and care inside yourself, you will eventually get burnt up.

To be the Two that everyone wants around, you need to learn to take better care of yourself. No one likes to be left cleaning a burnt pan, now, do they?

Red Flags to Watch Out for: Some red flags include people-pleasing and trying too hard to make people like you. You might go along with things you're not comfortable with, just so you can share something with others. Two is the child that always gives you their favorite toys just so you would play with them.

If you find yourself wearing clothes that you don't feel good in, or pretending to like things just because your partner or friend does, take a step back and reevaluate your real needs. It is good to be supportive, but going too far on the pleasing side will make you lose your true self.

Self-Development Activities: Going about their life focused on what other people want and need, it is pretty obvious that to boost self-development, Two needs to shift their attention to themselves a bit more. Here are some activities that will help Twos unleash their healthier side.

Love Yourself — Twos are either preoccupied with thinking too low of themselves — not being worthy enough for others to care for them — or with having a pretty high view — the martyr who always takes care of others and never gets anything in return. Try not to go to extremes. This may feel like walking on a rope without falling on either side, but reminding yourself of your good and bad traits will help you maintain the balance.

For instance, grab a piece of paper and divide it into two equal parts. On the left side, write down the things you believe are good about you. On the right, write down what you think to be your faults. When you notice yourself getting angry at others for not returning the amount of love and care you've invested in them, just go over your faults and remind yourself that you are not perfect, either. When you feel not good enough, read aloud the things you excel at and let them punch you back to reality. This will help you learn to love yourself for who you are.

Practice Self-Care — Self-care is probably the most important thing you need to pay attention to as a Type 2. This can apply to all levels: physically, emotionally, mentally, and spiritually. Acknowledging and nurturing your needs can keep your energy level in check, supporting the healthy side of your personality.

The self-care activities can be as simple as treating yourself with a box of chocolates, scheduling a massage, and buying that nice dress you've just spotted. Or they can run more deeply and include quitting a job that makes you feel bad, moving to your dream house, and making life changes based on what will make *you* feel better.

Check In with Your Emotions — It may be in your nature to put other people's needs first, but you need to remind yourself that you have feelings, as well. And yes, they matter just the same (if not even more!) than those of the people around you. So, make it a habit to check in with your emotions and see how you're feeling at given moments.

For instance, three or four times a day, stop what you are doing and ask yourself, *How am I doing at this moment? What do I need to feel better?* It is even wise to set a reminder so you don't forget. Because, being a Two, trust me, you will forget to check in with yourself. It's also important to hold back sometimes when you're trying to help others. Why? Because what you think they need might not be what they really need. When you're forceful in this way, others can find it overbearing.

Become more aware of your motives for helping others as well. Is it because you want to give to them? Or is it because you want them to appreciate you? If it's the latter, find a way to feel fulfilled within yourself, first and foremost.

Doing Your Best in Relationships — Your relationships with others can improve when you release them from your rigorous expectations. For example, not everyone shows appreciation in the same ways, especially those personality types whose focus is less on lavish displays of emotion and sentiment. If you can look beyond the ways you expect others to respond in this regard, you may realize they have completely different intentions that you originally thought. Here are some tips to follow:

- When you notice yourself feeling a little bit overwhelmed by your urge to help someone, ask yourself if that is really expected of you. Is it your job to do that? You may even want to discuss this with another friend.
- Learn to say NO. You don't have to help everyone at any time and at any cost. You may think this will strengthen your relationships, but it will only take a huge portion of your energy, leaving you hurt in the end. Saying NO, as horrible as it may sound to you now, can actually be healthy. Try it sometimes.
- Express your thoughts and needs. Stop feeling like your needs will thwart your connection with other people. Being honest in what you want will eliminate guesswork and help the people around you to understand the real you better.

Thriving at Work — Twos are the power behind the leader. They are second in command and the right hand of the ruler. They do their best to help the business thrive without having any aspirations to take over the throne. They are fine with assisting those in charge — in fact, having a powerful figure that relies on their opinion and advice makes them happy. However, for Twos to really excel in the workplace, they need to follow these three rules:

1. Don't be afraid to take the lead — You don't always need to let those from a higher hierarchy level reap all the benefits. You, too, deserve to be allowed to do the best you can. Whenever you see an opportunity for it, take the initiative.
2. Cut back on flattering powerful people just so that you will remain likable.
3. Let your coworkers know they can count on you, but don't let them take advantage of your Two personality — avoid helping others when that interferes with your schedule.

Jobs and Career Paths: Nursing, social work, counseling, childcare, or anything where care is a significant component. You might suit teaching, especially younger children that may need more emotional support. Perhaps you'd even suit being a massage therapist, a physiotherapist, or a paramedic. Service is the key aspect of careers that suit Type 2s.

The jobs that a Two wouldn't be too successful at are those that involve harsh criticism or telling people what to do, but not in a good way. Those are usually the professions that are not very likable such as tax auditor, editor, literary agent, college admissions officer, etc.

Activities and Hobbies: It goes without saying that you enjoy spending time with others, socializing. You probably like spending time with animals as well. You might choose to volunteer for a cause or community project. Maybe you would like to help your neighbors with jobs around the house or garden.

SPIRITUALITY

Spiritual Struggles: Twos will be there to listen and care for you without any strings attached. Well, almost! The only thing they need in return is for you to depend on their love and help. Which is pretty impossible not to! But even though the bond is strong, Twos still have trouble unleashing their true self and hide behind their fear of being rejected. They will not talk about their sorrows, always wearing their cheerful mask. This can be quite a struggle.

My Two friend, even after all these years, still doesn't like to talk about her problems or share discomforting situations with me. She would rather just sit and listen to me whine about my messy schedule, reassuring me that I couldn't possibly get any more perfect (me being a One says it all, I guess).

If you are a Loving Assistant, then I guess this section has been a painful reality punch for you. But don't worry, the only thing you need to do is take a step back, breathe deeply, and learn that It's okay to show a little bit more of yourself to others.

Your Life Lesson and the Path of Integration: Love is unconditional in its truest form. It doesn't depend on anyone's actions, it just *is*. Learn that love does not depend on giving and receiving. The amount you give or receive is not an indicator of your own worth. You can learn to celebrate others' happiness without having to have contributed to it — others can be happy without depending on your help, and you can be okay with that.

Also, learning to allow others to give is an important part of the path. If you don't allow others to give, you rob them of the opportunity to experience the joy of giving that you also seek. Keep in mind that, while it's admirable for us all to help each other, we are ultimately responsible for ourselves. This frees you from needing others and allows you to free others from feeling overwhelmed by your desire to help them.

Daily Affirmations and Transformations for Type Twos:

- I NOW LET GO of the feeling that I am cast aside and unwanted
- I NOW ACCEPT that people love me for who I am
- I NOW LET GO of being clingy and overly dependent on others
- I NOW ACCEPT that is okay to let others go their own way
- I NOW LET GO craving attention for the things I'm doing for others
- I NOW ACCEPT that helping others is not what builds my happiness
- I NOW LET GO of flattering others to get them to like me
- I NOW ACCEPT that is okay to work on my growth and development to be a better person
- I NOW LET GO of expecting others to read my mind and know what I need
- I NOW ACCEPT that I should express myself better and be clearer about my motives

COMPATIBILITY — HOW WELL "TWO" SUITS THE OTHER TYPES

Type 1: One and Two may seem like quite the match at first since they're both interested in helping others. One focused on the greater good or their mission, and Two having a strong urge to serve other people. However, the thing that these two types share in common — their inability to express their needs — may pose a serious threat to the future of this relationship. Both One and Two will need to work on letting the other half know how they feel if they want this to work.

Type 2: Two Type 2s understand each other's desire to have their needs met and to give and receive emotionally. This can make for a very positive foundation for a relationship. They are both invested in ensuring the wellbeing of the relationship and each other. Because of this dynamic, jealousy can arise if one partner also seeks social interaction from other people outside of the relationship.

Type 3: This pair can complement each other very well. Threes like receiving attention and Twos like giving it. Threes bring a practical edge to the relationship, helping to balance the emotional world of Type 2. Twos can, however, feel that a Three's focus on success means they are not prioritizing the relationship.

Type 4: Again, this can be a very good combination, as both types are able to give to each other emotionally.

Fours can be a positive influence, in the sense that they encourage Twos to become more self-aware and explore their emotional worlds in a deeper way.

Type 5: Type Fives can find relationships difficult, which is why they become super loyal when they make a promising connection. They're also good listeners. Naturally, this suits Type 2s. Fives provide emotional stability, and they enjoy the attention that Twos give them.

Type 6: A relationship between a Type 2 and Six has a foundation of trust and dependability. They both treat their commitment to each other as very important. Twos should be mindful that Sixes can perceive unwanted advice as intrusive and undermining their confidence. If a Six wants your help, they will make sure you are aware of it.

Type 7: Type 7 is a positive influence on Two because they remind them to check their own needs and take care of themselves. Since both types are friendly and enjoy connection, together they can be very welcoming to their community. Sevens may be pushed away by a Type 2 if they become clingy, as Sevens have a free-spirited nature.

Type 8: Type 8s are very practical. This brings balance to the emotional world of the Type 2. While Eights are able to pay attention to the Two's personal needs, they can be seen as cold, since they respect autonomy and have a different attitude toward dealing with people in general.

Type 9: Type 9s are calm and easy-going. They can reassure Type 2s about their doubts and offer acceptance. Both types seek support, and the greatest thing about this combo is that they are actually able to provide for each other. Conflict can arise since neither can share their feelings in a healthy well. Nines usually don't speak up, but once they do, the dissatisfaction that has been piling up inside can force Two to lash out emotionally.

MISIDENTIFICATION

Sometimes people confuse Type 2s and 3s. They both want others to like them but the key is that they have very different ways of doing so. Threes focus less on the other person, gaining others' interest through their own self-mastery. The ambition of Threes may also be seen as selfish from a Two's perspective. It's also quite common to mistake a Two for a Six. They seek to connect with others but the thing is, they again have a completely different way of going about it. Sixes form bonds through being playful and they're more selective about who they connect with. They're also more likely to feel stifled than Twos, and they're less nurturing.

AN OUTSIDER'S GUIDE TO TYPE 2S

To get along with me, you should understand why I might get angry if I feel taken advantage of. It's just because it's happened so much in the past, and I assume other people are going to be unappreciative. It's not always something to take personally. If you push me away for seeming clingy, it only makes things worse. I like having the opportunity to give to others. Giving me your time and energy so that I can give back to you is what satisfies me the most.

The best way to resolve conflict with me is to first allow me to express my needs. I tend to avoid conflict and this makes it harder to recognize and resolve problems, so I need to feel safe in saying this.

Type 3

The Rainmaker

At their BEST:

successful
good-looking
energetic
confident
efficient
charming
ambitious

At their WORST:

approval-seeking
insincere
arrogant
overly competitive
superficial
narcissistic
workaholic

Shareable Quote:

There isn't a task too hard to complete;
I do my best to win — I get motivated when I compete.
I aim high to reach the top, I'll do anything,
even personalities I swap.
Please forgive if sometimes I sound like a jerk,
but I mean all well, I'm just too stressed with work.

3.3 TYPE 3

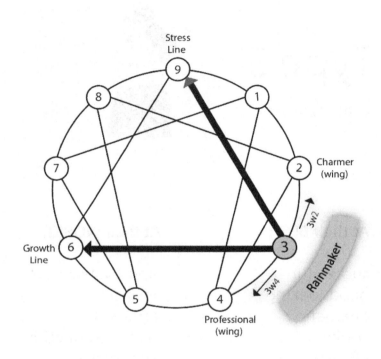

Enneagram Diagram for Type Three

N **ame:** Type 3 — The Rainmaker

AKA: The Charming Motivator, The Status Seeker, The Successful Professional, The Ambitious Performer, The Workaholic

Personality: Three is the type of person that could turn any boring activity into a hypercompetitive situation. And I'm talking about Monica-Geller-from-*Friends* kind of competitive. Like that episode, when she and Rachel entered a large-scale trivia bet and ended up losing their apartment. Except a Three would actually force Joey and Chandler to get rid of their birds and keep the apartment. Because that's what Threes do. They transform, enhance, and achieve. Three is the guy you call when you need to turn some tables around. Because guess what? That's what they're best at!

Do you know that saying *He could sell sand to an Arab?* Well, I guess you could think of Threes as the inspiration behind it. Because no matter how challenging a task is if you need it accomplished, just give it to Three. Threes are ambitious, goal-oriented, and push hard to come out as winners.

If you are a Type 3, you're very driven, energetic, competent, and accomplished. Status is important to you, so you make sure you do the right things to get the achievements that will make others admire and praise you. You can be a wonderful role model that others look up to. You want to "have it all," but this does not only mean being a competitive workaholic — you can even get mercenary if people are standing in the way of your advancement.

If Threes were an animal, they would have been chameleons. Always changing their appearance to fit into different situations so they could come out on top. But, while this sounds like a good thing on a professional level,

Threes are at risk of losing connection with their inner nature while being so busy polishing the outer shell.

At your best, you're a true inspiration to others and achieve greatness. At your worst, you get desperate for attention and are unable to accept failure as a possibility, making you come off as mean.

Your Worst Fear: That your mask will finally come off and that others will see that the real you is less worthy than what they initially assumed. Your biggest fear is being unable to come out as a winner in the eyes of other people.

Your Heart's Desire: To be successful and valued by others. You live to look good, so the thing that makes you the happiest is being perceived as someone who has it all figured out.

Your Biggest Sin: Being a *poseur*, a phony — Three is the type of person who would slay the job interview and then excuse themselves to the bathroom, just so they could *google* what the job actually entails.

Wings:

3w2 The Charmer — You have amazing personal warmth and charisma, which helps you achieve your goals and status. You have a lust for attention and success, and that is what drives you most days. Some days though, when you let your ambitions overtake you, you can start feeling unappreciated and even get hostile. You think that your value is established by your accomplishments, and you struggle to accept when you hit a roadblock. You are the employee of the month, and you have a charm that attracts other people like a magnet.

3w4 The Professional — You throw yourself into your career as a measure of success but may leave your own true personality behind. Compared with 3w2, the w4 gives you restraint to act in a more controlled and pulled-together way. You think before you speak, are highly practical, and incredibly efficient in completing tasks. You are the real expert in your line of work, and you are mostly focused on working on your personal growth and improvement. The Four wing is what pulls you back when you go just a bit too far on the confident side, but even though you may not be the star in the room like 3w2, you can still be perceived as pretentious.

Subtypes:

Self-preservation Type 3 — The Company Man/Woman (the countertype)

You perform exceptionally, you have the right image, and you're a huge success at work. *Security* is your middle name, and you have a strong need to be self-sufficient and provide for yourself and others. Perhaps this can be a result of a struggling childhood that lacked protection. You were the kind of student that always finished early and had time to help the person sitting next to you. You are the countertype because, despite your professional aspirations, you go against your vanity. You actually express it by being a supportive and charming assistant — a true company person.

Social Type 3 — The Politician

You get to know the right people and win power and admiration in the right circles. You're a smooth talker and have numerous connections and acquaintances. You're a person of huge respect, but beneath that shiny and polished outlook, you sometimes struggle to find real substance. You aim for prestige and the "applause" of others, and your competitive nature is mostly concerned with winning. You were the kind of child who liked to hang out with the older cool crew and craved their acceptance. Out of all Threes, the social one fears being perceived as not-worthy-enough the most.

Sexual Type 3 — The Movie Star

You're drawn to being either hypermasculine if you're a man, or hyperfeminine if you're a woman. You want to be exceptionally attractive to the opposite sex and embody the best things about your gender. Underneath, you may feel confused about your sexuality, or as though your sexuality is the only important part of you. You are a natural performer, which bodes well in many careers, but you also find it hard to find the "off" switch. You sometimes feel like you are playing a role in your pre-scripted relationships rather than pouring your soul into forming a real bond and actually experiencing it.

Stress Number: 9. When you're under stress and not feeling good, you take on the traits of unhealthy Nine. You can get very apathetic and lackluster. You can't get motivated and wonder what the point of everything is. You withdraw, numb out your emotions, and slip into daydreams. You often lose interest in going out, working out, following a healthy eating plan, and don't pay that much attention to your appearance.

Growth Number: 6. When you're in a good place, you jump to the sunny side of Six. You become more committed to others. You think more about other people close to you, and start to value your relationships. You are less blinkered by work and achievement and feel more generous and open-hearted. The urge to hold all the strings subsides, and you no longer feel the need to be admired or keep playing that hotshot role.

Center: Just like Two, Three also belongs in the Heart Center, where Shame and Emotion are what drives your being. This may seem counterproductive, as you would rather *do* feelings than *have* them, but you *feel* deeply, even though you seem out of touch with your center. Your fear of being seen as unworthy is a powerful emotion.

Famous 3s: Emperor Constantine, Prince William, Tony Robbins, Elvis Presley, Lance Armstrong, Madonna, Whitney Houston, Lady Gaga, Taylor Swift, Tom Cruise, Oprah Winfrey, Arnold Schwarzenegger, Courtney Cox, Michael Jordan, Demi Moore, Will Smith, Sylvester Stallone, Sharon Stone, Serena Williams, Reese Witherspoon, Beyoncé.

Shareable Quote: *There isn't a task too hard to complete; I do my best to win — I get motivated when I compete. I aim high to reach the top, I'll do anything, even personalities I swap. Please forgive me if sometimes I sound like a jerk, but I mean well, I'm just too stressed with work.*

MY INNER WORLD

What I Like About Being this Type: I like having ambition and drive. I like the fact that I'm working toward something great and constantly creating new goals. I love to work on self-improvement — I am motivated to grow and learn more when the finish line gets blurry and the outcome is uncertain. I actually love being challenged, because that's what pushes me to become better at what I am doing.

What's Hard About Being this Type: It can be exhausting at times. Often, I realize I've neglected my other needs when it's too late — meaning I'm already tired and burnt out. Prevention is better than cure, but I get so caught up in my projects that it doesn't always happen this way. Being so ambitious can create conflicting feelings because I actually love pleasing myself. I just barely find the time with my hectic schedule and busy days.

Your Personal Vices (addictions): Workaholism, working out too much, taking stimulants to keep pushing forward, always wanting to get more done. Your obsession with physical appearance can lead to abnormal amounts of cosmetic procedures or even cosmetic surgery. Imbalanced or heavily restricted diets are also a possibility.

Typical Thinking Patterns: I'm always thinking about what I need to do next to get ahead. I can get pretty obsessed with how I come across to others and look for ways to impress them to think of me as the I-don't-know-how-she/he-does-it kind of person.

Typical Feeling Patterns: When I'm doing well, I feel fulfilled and grateful for my progress. I'm happy and confident and enjoy the success I've created for myself. When I'm not doing so well, I can become anxious and fearful of failure.

SELF-DEVELOPMENT

When You're Very Healthy (levels 1 to 3): You accept and value yourself for who you are, not just your accomplishments. You believe in your own value, and you help others see their own worth, too. You're someone other people aspire to be, but that's not because of an image you're putting out; it's because of who you *really* are.

You operate at your peak, and you're self-motivated and self-assured. You achieve things that inspire others and can be a great role model. You know what you have to offer, and you believe in your ability to deliver and succeed. Your self-esteem is high and things just get better and better for you.

When You're Very Unhealthy (levels 7 to 9): When in a bad place, you feel like a failure, and you can even hate or envy other people for their success. You will sabotage others and betray them if it helps you to advance. You feel jealous as if someone else's success is a personal insult to you. At the most extreme, Narcissistic Personality Disorder and psychopathic tendencies are seen in Type 3s.

When You're Somewhere in Between (levels 4 to 6): You may be very concerned with how others perceive you. You seek success, not because of the goal, but because of wanting to be the best and beat others. Others may see you as insincere, arrogant, and attention-seeking.

How to Maximize Your Potential: Find balance by getting adequate rest. People don't get ahead by losing sleep — they make their best choices when their mind is sharp. A good night's sleep gives you plenty of energy to perform at your best. Keep your focus on your true, authentic goals, instead of getting sidetracked by your appearance to the external world.

Red Flags to Watch Out for: Obsession with achievement can lead to self-neglect. You may place so much importance on the future that you forget to enjoy the present moment. This also has an existential component to it, where you can feel empty without having a goal. You may experience fear of failure and push yourself to extremes to succeed. You might be a workaholic or burnout. You can even find yourself playing a shape-shifting role — changing your wants and needs so you can fit into the environment.

Self-Development Activities: As a Three who spends all of their time just doing and doing, it is pretty obvious that your being craves a step back and a slower pace. For you to establish self-awareness and work on your inner development, you need to find activities that will work against your controlling and image-polishing nature.

Practice Solitude — Everyone needs rest, but practicing solitude is especially important for Threes, as they are highly active, mostly focused on productivity. Make it a habit to set aside just 10 or 15 minutes a day to simply sit in silence, without placing your attention on anything in particular. This may include sitting in the park and observing the greenery, or even practicing meditation to quiet your racing mind.

Avoid Bringing Your Work Home — Working even when they're not working is a habit that Threes have to shake off. Unless you have some super-important project you need to work on, don't prioritize everything. Find time to relax after working hours, and avoid talking about your job as well. Not being constantly reminded of your aspirations and goals can help you loosen up.

Try Holding Your Tongue — You don't always have to be in charge. Sometimes, even if it is super tempting to share your opinion and give suggestions, try holding your tongue and avoid leading. Let someone else take the wheel for once while you're blending with the crowd.

Re-evaluate the Meaning of Success — Grab a piece of paper and write down what you think success is. Then, go over what you've written very carefully, and try to see if this truly aligns with how you feel. Is your definition of success really yours? Or is it something that you've inherited or you think is expected of you? Do this when you're alone to avoid unconsciously shaping your answer for others. If your so-called success doesn't quite match what you really desire and believe to be valuable, take your feelings into consideration and craft a brand new definition. Then try to stick to it!

Doing Your Best in Relationships — Being so busy presenting the best image of your relationship/family to the outer world can seriously exhaust your partner/friend/kids and push your bond downhill... Here are some other tips that can help you keep your urge for polishing the exterior at bay:

- Stop aiming for all things ideal. Your relationship is not an Instagram post, so don't make it feel like everything should be staged and ready to take the spotlight. Mess in smaller doses is actually rewarding. Try it sometimes.

- Find a person that you can be truly vulnerable with. As a Three, you probably have many people you meet with daily, but choose the one that you trust the most. This can either be your partner, a close friend, or a family member. Take off your I-know-best mask in their presence, and allow yourself to just be yourself. You can survive being less than *the best* with one person. Try it out.

- Be reminded of who you really are. Being so busy polishing your best version can make you forget about what the *actual you* really needs. And, if you lose touch with yourself, how can you connect with someone else? If it helps, write down some vulnerable things about yourself, and read them every night before going to bed. This will help you form friendships that really matter.

Thriving at Work — Three is already thriving in the workplace. But at whose expense? You may be at the top of your game, but that is not in line with the real you that you're hiding inside. To really be satisfied with your job, try to focus on your accomplishments, not on setbacks. Not only is this good for your self-esteem, but it's also necessary for success. Some of the most successful entrepreneurs have had a ton of roadblocks — it is what's made them successful. Try to follow these three rules:

1. Develop authenticity by reflecting on *why* you want to be successful in your chosen field. This helps to keep things in perspective by putting you back in touch with what your true motivation is.
2. When you're racing toward the finish line, be mindful of what happens to the coworkers left behind. You may want to reach the top, but you don't have to step on others to get there. Find your own path.
3. Take frequent vacations and try not to work as much. Your personal life will thank you for it.

Jobs and Career Paths: Business, management, any career with good prospects or a path for getting to the top of your game. Threes can be excellent lawyers, producers, journalists, etc. Acting and performing arts are also popular choices for Threes, as their need to be *the star* motivates them to be better.

Three's worst career would be anything that doesn't have a clear path toward advancements. That might include having an online store or working as a freelancer.

Activities and Hobbies: You're likely to pass the time doing things that will contribute to your success since Threes are all about developing their skills. Whatever your area of interest is, you'll probably spend time mastering it wherever you can. Whether it's a case of sport, dancing, singing, or anything else, you want to achieve success and your spare time is time to use to move toward it. Engaging in personal development is also very important to Type 3s.

SPIRITUALITY

Spiritual Struggles: Focusing so much on the future that you ignore the present moment — the moment where your *life* is happening! Just like Type 1s, you need to *do* less and *be* more. Life is more than just a to-do list.

You can be loved and accepted despite your external success. Your worth does not depend on what you achieve or "getting it right." It might be a difficult path, but one day, you can realize that you were just fine all along, just the way you are.

Your Life Lesson and the Path of Integration: Your value does not depend on anything outside of you. This includes how others perceive you. It can be a struggle, but finally, you may get to the point where you realize that failure is not necessarily what you think it is.

You may have already been successful in many ways. You may have overcome many things, and that in itself is a form of achievement. Even if you don't accomplish your greatest ambition in its ultimate perfectionist form, it doesn't mean you have failed.

You were seeking to perfect your external image so much, when in fact, being yourself was always enough. Chasing approval was never necessary.

Daily Affirmations and Transformations for Type Threes:

- I NOW LET GO of my need to measure my value through my achievements
- I NOW ACCEPT that I am worthy, regardless of my accomplishments
- I NOW LET GO of detaching myself from my feelings in order to succeed
- I NOW ACCEPT listening to my needs and emotions more closely
- I NOW LET GO of the need to always be at the top
- I NOW ACCEPT allowing others to lead *me* sometimes
- I NOW LET GO of getting jealous of the success of others
- I NOW ACCEPT that I should be happy with what I've got

- I NOW LET GO of my fear of revealing my real self to others
- I NOW ACCEPT that I will be happier if I show a piece of my soul to someone else

COMPATIBILITY — HOW WELL "THREE" SUITS THE OTHER TYPES

Type 1: Ones and Threes are both highly driven, so there's less chance of their work commitments becoming an issue with each other. One won't mind Three working on a project until 2 a.m., while Three will be totally okay with One trying on a dress for the umpteenth time to get the perfect look. Threes help Type 1s be less perfectionist. They both prefer to handle things practically rather than emotionally, so this helps deal with conflict.

Type 2: As I mentioned before, this combination can be a good basis for a relationship. A Type 3 will have genuine support from a Type 2 and is someone that will always be proud and supportive of their achievements.

Type 3: Two Type 3s together, when they are functioning at their optimum, can be an unstoppable force. They can motivate and encourage each other, and they give each other space to pursue their goals. If they have a family, they should ensure that they don't neglect their other responsibilities, since they are both so focused on their professional or other goals.

Type 4: Another good combination. Fours can help Threes to develop greater self-awareness and to understand their emotions on a deeper level. Fours can encourage them to appreciate the richness of the present moment and to enjoy the less-practical aspects of life.

Type 5: Type 5s understand Type 3s desire for professional mastery and they are supportive of it. They allow each other space, and like when two Type 3s are together, their similar approach to handling emotions allows them to resolve issues with mutual respect.

Type 6: Both types are action-oriented, hard workers. Type 6s have a compassionate quality about them. They may help Type 3s that have more superficial tendencies to focus more on others, such as those that are in need.

Type 7: Both are energetic, optimistic, and sociable, so this is a good foundation. However, the Type 7s definition of success is quite different from the Type 3s. They have a much more relaxed approach to what it means to be successful, so they may be dissatisfied if they have to sacrifice a fun night out just so Three can go through that work project one more time.

Type 8: An Eight can encourage a Three to be more in touch with their emotions. This is because Type 8s are very strong and sturdy, allowing the Three to let their guard down. Both types are assertive, whereas Type 3s are

3.3 TYPE 3 | 137

more diplomatic about it. So, this can be a good combination in business, as well as in relationships.

Type 9: Similar to Type 4s, Nines can help Threes to relax and enjoy more of the simple things in the present moment. They are also very supportive of Threes, and their easy-going demeanor brings balance to the Three's vigor. They teach the Three that they can be loved just as they are, and their worth is not based on their achievements.

MISIDENTIFICATION

A common misidentification is with Type 8s. Both types are driven, highly ambitious, and intend to get what they want. They both want to rise to success and they're competitive. A key difference between the two is that Eights care a lot less about what others think. They want to get what they want, period. They're not doing it so that others will admire them or approve of them. Type 8s are also more driven by power. This is not the driving force for Type 3s.

AN OUTSIDER'S GUIDE TO TYPE 3S

You can get along with me by knowing that I always prioritize my ambitions. I might not always be available if I have something important to do that contributes to my long-term goals. It's likely that I'll be working a lot, so don't take it personally — I'm unavailable to most people a lot of the time. Less fun and more work to secure a good future is my motto.

To resolve conflicts with me, it's best to keep emotion out of it. I prefer to be practical and get straight to business. I like people to be direct with me, no beating around the bush or dropping hints. I like things to be clearly communicated to me to set things straight in the quickest, easiest way possible.

Avoid talking to me in a judgmental way — I will probably react badly if I feel like I'm under criticism. I prefer feedback in a form that's calm and doesn't suggest that someone thinks they know better than me. I will only get competitive and try to beat you in your own game.

Type 4

The Rock Star

At their BEST:

creative
bohemian
unique
artistic
sensitive
intuitive
talented

At their WORST:

melodramatic
depressive
temperamental
emotional
self-absorbed
moralistic
withdrawn

Shareable Quote:

I feel at home when I am sad,
but I am just unique — I am not mad.
If you choose left, I will go right;
the artist in me loves to stand out, I paint, dream, write.
When emotions overwhelm, I become a touch dramatic,
my free and creative spirit leads the way,
I am anything but static.

3.4 TYPE 4

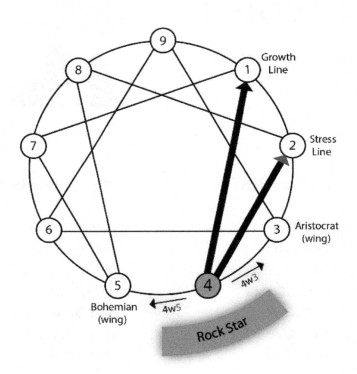

Enneagram Diagram for Type Four

Name: Type 4 — The Rock Star

AKA: The Romantic, The Creative, The Artist, The Bohemian, The Melancholic

Personality: Four was probably that goth/emo kid in your class, with the all-black clothes, deadpan expression, and the-world-doesn't-get-me attitude. Fours go through their life not quite fitting, always feeling unique and misunderstood by others. And they are totally fine with that — being like the rest of the world scares them to death. They are often doing the opposite of what others are doing, which can sometimes make them seem aloof. The truth? Fours are not weirdos, they are just creatively different. I'm talking about van-Gogh kind of different.

When I started my road to self-discovery, I also began talking all things Enneagram with, well, pretty much everyone I knew. From recommending articles to, "Why won't you just find the time to do the test — it's life-changing," the people around me felt kind of obligated to give it a try. One day, one of my closest friends gave me a call and said, "It turns out I am not hormonal all the time — I am just a classic Type Four."

Fours can feel like they're on a never-ending emotional rollercoaster. They can jump from melancholy to melo-drama in a matter of seconds, and they represent the most complex, multiple-layered Enneagram type. Their "Why am I feeling this way," can shortly turn into "What is the purpose of the Universe?" If there was a movie about a Four, it would be shot in England or somewhere gray and cloudy, with Erik Satie's "Gymnopédies" playing in the background.

If you are a Type 4, you're very aware of your feelings and you have a rich inner world. You are emotionally honest and sincere, and very empathetic to others when they're suffering. But you can also be self-conscious, especially when it comes to situations where there is little to no emotional depth. You hate the superficial, the utilitarian, and the false. You're searching for beauty, truth, and uniqueness.

At your best, you create beauty and uniqueness wherever you go, transforming ugliness and suffering into beauty and hope. At your worst, you can be very self-indulgent and feel like you're so uniquely flawed that no one can understand you. Your suffering can make you selfish, and you can even be addicted to this suffering.

Your Worst Fear: That you have no identity, that you are nothing. Four feels like there is an essential part of them missing. Like there is an INCOMPLETE sign written on their forehead, warning other people to stay away from them. They want to join the show of life, but they cannot find the ticket to enter. Their inability to find meaning in their existence makes them feel like outcasts, expelled from the rest of the world.

Your Heart's Desire: To create your significance to yourself and to the world, to leave your unique mark. Four's artistic and genuine nature is what separates them from the normalcy in which the rest of the world functions and makes them special. Their biggest passion is to be able to leave something creative behind and be recognized through greatness.

Your Biggest Sin: Being envious. Four struggles to find comfort in the things which seem to make other people happy. They often feel left out and isolated, not worthy enough to fit the mold. This works for them just fine, until they reach the point in which they start envying others for moving through life with such ease they can never possibly achieve. It's almost like a little orphan pressed against the window of a happy home, observing the warmth and security of another family, longing for something they know they will never have. This envy is not just wanting to have something, though — it becomes a deep melancholy and a powerful urge to suffer.

Wings:

4w3 The Aristocrat — You place yourself apart from society and gain your uniqueness by putting yourself _above others_. Just like a Three, you aim for the top, which in your Four's nature means becoming the one with the most special talents. You are part of the elite and may have very high-end tastes, manners, and aesthetics. Socially, you are more accepted than the other Fours, but being more easy-going around people, for a Four, usually means being more melodramatic. Thanks to the Three's workaholic tendencies, these Fours are more productive, but they are usually the ones that are prone to becoming emotional trainwrecks.

4w5 The Bohemian — You place yourself apart by moving *outside of the society*. You despise anything conventional, and your goal is to reach extreme uniqueness, which often turns Fours into eccentrics. You do not fit into any social category, nor do you want to. You'd rather create your own identity and be one of a kind. If you have to decide between a paid vacation with a friend in the Bahamas or a week in the rainy English countryside alone, you will choose the latter in a heartbeat. You love spending time on your own and letting your emotions take over completely, without having to talk about or act on them.

Subtypes:

Self-preservation Type 4 — The Masochistic Artist (the countertype)

You travel far and wide, toward wherever authenticity beckons. You have multiple moves across houses and countries, and many changes in lifestyle and career. Other people may see you as reckless and chaotic. Sometimes this may be the case, but it can also be a great adventurous life, both in the inner and outer world. In many cases, these Fours have trouble identifying themselves as Fours, because they would endure their suffering rather than showing their wounded soul to the world. Self-preservation Fours are more stoic, and instead of reaching melancholic depths, they turn to masochism. Sometimes the pull between society and authenticity overwhelms them, other times, that's what makes them feel good.

Social Type 4 — The Shameful Critic

You want status and belonging, but they feel hard to find. This makes you feel envious of others who seem to win these easily, and you feel deficient. You seek to define your role, often by analyzing others' behaviors and motives and possibly criticizing them. You feel a need to be your authentic self, and also to belong to a group, and it can be hard to square these. You feel a strong need to be seen in your suffering, and sometimes believe that once others see your pain, they will forgive you for your deficiencies. The social Four is the type of person that bursts into tears easily and has the strongest attachment to their suffering because they find their pain to be the only real thing in life.

Sexual Type 4 — The Free Spirit

You don't feel powerful or worthy, but you really want to get to the place where you do. When you see other people being strong or successful, you take it as a personal challenge to help you exert your own authority and build your own power. This becomes your mission, and your self-worth rises and falls depending on how you measure up to others. You don't really care about being recognized by normal people, but you want to be acknowledged by those *insiders* or *elite* who are in-the-know about the sphere in which you're working. Anger is a common sensation with sexual Fours, and despite their sense of being inferior, they usually come off as arrogant. They crave emotional intensity and are very direct about what they want and need.

Stress Number: 2. When you're under stress and not feeling good, you become clingy and over-involved with other people, resembling an unhealthy Two. You begin craving attention and acceptance from those around you at the expense of your true needs. If you feel that one person understands you in particular, you will become excessively dependent on them, and even allow jealousy to swoop in.

Growth Number: 1. When you're in a good place, you become less jealous and emotional, and more measured. You can see things more objectively, and everything doesn't feel as heavy. With the help of One's perfection-seeking tendencies, when you're feeling secure, you stop talking about your dreams and ideas and become down-to-earth enough to actually realize them and work on their accomplishment.

Center: You're in the Heart, Emotional, or Feeling Center. That means that you experience emotional shifts, and you have to work on regulating and stabilizing your feelings. It may be hard for a Four to detach from the emotions as this type is used to acting on their feelings in an impulsive, almost- exaggerated manner. You embrace your center and focus your feelings inward — you concentrate on how you feel.

Famous 4s: Amy Winehouse, Prince, Nicolas Cage, Prince Charles, Michael Jackson, Angelina Jolie, Michelangelo, Rumi, Johnny Depp, Vincent van Gogh, Julio Iglesias, Marilyn Manson, Edith Piaf, Johnny Depp, Naomi Campbell.

Shareable Quote: *I feel at home when I am sad, but I am just unique — I am not mad. If you choose left, I will go right; the artist in me loves to stand out, I paint, dream, write. When emotions overwhelm, I become a touch dramatic, my free and creative spirit leads the way, I am anything but static.*

MY INNER WORLD

What I Like About Being this Type: I enjoy experimenting with my imagination, dreaming up all kinds of wonderful things. I like immersing myself in creativity and expressing myself through it. The inspiration invigorates me. Being true to myself matters, and I like the experience of re-inventing myself. I actually feel comfortable when I'm melancholic, and the fact that I am not like everybody else powers my existence.

What's Hard About Being this Type: It can be isolating and confusing. It can feel like something is wrong or missing in my life, and I'm not sure exactly what to do to fill that void. I can't just ignore my emotions either, which makes it hard to function in a world that's filled with responsibilities. I'm not someone who can just put on a brave face and ignore my feelings, which can get quite intense at times.

Your Personal Vices (addictions): Mood-altering substances like alcohol. Alcohol also helps with socializing when it feels difficult to do so. Psychedelic drugs to enhance the self-created fantasy world. Cosmetic surgery or obsession with physical appearance to compensate for perceived defects.

Typical Thinking Patterns: Introspective, always asking questions about myself and trying to explore who I am and understand myself better. Sometimes my thoughts are painfully self-critical. Otherwise, I'm dreaming up new creative ideas and exploring my imagination.

Typical Feeling Patterns: I can experience mood swings and intense emotions. Sometimes they're overwhelming, and it can take a while to start to feel better. There can be overtones of longing, but it's hard to realize what I'm actually longing for. My positive emotions are often based on feeling inspired by new ideas and being enthusiastic about working on them.

SELF-DEVELOPMENT

When You're Very Healthy (levels 1 to 3): You are extremely creative in numerous ways. You create physical beauty around you, but you're also genuine on a mental, emotional, and physical level — you can take negative experiences and feelings and transform them into expressions of abundance and beauty. You're highly sensitive and intuitive to yourself and others, and meet your own deeper needs and those of other people.

When You're Very Unhealthy (levels 7 to 9): When in a bad place, you feel like the worst person in the world. You absolutely despise yourself for reasons that don't really make sense, and everyday life feels intensely painful. You blame others and drive them away, and you feel forced to jump on the suffering train.

When You're Somewhere in Between (levels 4 to 6): At this level, you take things more personally than if you were functioning at healthier levels. You are more likely to withdraw and become hypersensitive. Self-pity may take over, leaving you unproductive and melancholic.

How to Maximize Your Potential: Find ways to manage your feelings to prevent them from taking over your life. Once you find a way to step out of the emotional tornado, you can put your amazing creativity to good use and function at your peak. Believe in yourself and develop confidence in the great talents you have to offer.

Red Flags to Watch Out for: Negative moods triggered by imagined, negative scenarios or conversations. A constant feeling of hopelessness or despair and frequently questioning your identity. Feeling isolated from everyone else, or that nobody could possibly understand you.

Self-Development Activities: For a Four, the biggest struggle is not having some structure in their life. They tend to "go with the flow," and that is what they think feeds their inspiration and makes them unique. But that is also what forces them to go into those darker corners of their soul. If you are a Four and you wish to grow emotionally, then you are in desperate need of some self-development changes.

Try Acting Before Obsessing — As much as you like to wait for inspiration to take over and put you in the right mood to become more productive, sometimes things don't work out that way. There's not always "the perfect moment" to take action. Focus less on the fear that things won't work out perfectly if you don't wait for the "right" time. Instead of going through scenarios in your head, try to actually do something about it, without focusing on the possible unwanted outcome so much. I am not talking about becoming reckless, obviously, but instead of waiting for the perfect rainy day to paint that picture, just take the darn brush and start creating *now*.

Practice Mindfulness — Mindfulness is the thing that drags the daydreamers back to reality. Practicing it can help you knock down the effect that the fantasies you're entertaining in your mind have on you. When you notice yourself imagining negative conversations and events, slowly bring your focus back to the present moment and the outer world. You can do this by including all of your senses. Try placing your attention on the things you can hear, see, feel, taste, smell. If you are in a park, focus on the smell of the freshly cut grass, the flowers, listen to the chirping of the birds, or the distant chattering. If you are in your room, focus on the silence, on the warmth. Be mindful of your surroundings.

Cut Back on the Suffering — Okay, so you're a Four and your suffering is the only real thing about you — I get it. But try to minimize it to decrease the negative effect it has on your whole being. When you notice yourself wallowing in the blues, grab a piece of paper and write down the reason for your pain. Below that reason, write down the cause for it. Once you figure out what causes your suffering, you will have a better idea of how to actually fix the issue. Write down possible solutions and try to be more problem-solving oriented.

Other activities that can help your personality grow include:

- Listening to other people's problems and realizing that you're not the only person in the world who is suffering
- Stop comparing yourself to others to keep envy at bay
- When you catch yourself dwelling in the past, write down the things that you want to achieve in the future to change your perspective

Doing Your Best in Relationships. Four feels that no one gets them so they tend to be social weirdos. If you've ever watched a Johnny Depp interview, then you know what I am talking about. As a Four, he clearly feels awkward when the TV host asks him a bunch of personal questions. And while he is a sweetheart (I cannot think of a woman who doesn't fancy him), it is clear that forming bonds doesn't come naturally to him. To stop that social awkwardness from getting in the way of your relationships, here are some tips for you to follow:

- Don't focus on what is lacking in the people you are with; instead, try to find the thing that makes them special.
- When your emotions start to pile up, bite your tongue to stop drama from happening. Not every quarrel should be stage-worthy.
- Stop assuming — just because you believe that you sound weird doesn't mean that's actually the case.
- Don't look for the meaning or beauty in every coffee date — sometimes, it is okay to *just chill and hang out.*

Thriving at Work — As a Four, you may be prone to skipping the secure gigs and look for the beauty of the uncertain and independent jobs. But, whatever turn you've taken on the career path, there are three rules your type should follow to thrive:

1. You are the best in your own way — don't compare your project, art, or style to anyone else's.
2. Avoid focusing on the ideal outcome of the finished work — sometimes it is okay to just see things through to completion.
3. When searching for meaning, don't go above and beyond — every job is meaningful in some way. Try to find the beauty in your profession.

Jobs and Career Paths: Fours thrive when able to do something that allows them to express themselves completely and allows their full potential to come to the surface. Writing, acting, music, or any career in the creative arts seems like the perfect job — from hair stylists and designers to tattoo artists. Fours make great masseuses or yoga instructors, as well.

The worst possible job for a Four would be anything that involves enforcing rules or standards to other people, such as police officers, stockbrokers, lawyers, or even jobs in the administrative world.

Activities and Hobbies: Creativity or whichever form of self-expression you enjoy. Maybe it's writing, art, music, or a combination of different activities. Whatever gives you that feeling of expression and the exhilaration of turning your inspiration into a physical outcome.

SPIRITUALITY

Spiritual Struggles: Knowing who you are. This is the underlying struggle Type 4s face. We could argue that this is a search that all humans undergo, but this is particularly intense with Fours. You don't need to try to be unique with every little thing that you're doing– keep in mind that no two humans share the same identity in this world, so you already are different than the rest of the world. Also, keep in mind that leaving your "special" mark isn't a gauge for your worthiness — you are worthy just the way you are.

Some Fours might also spend so much time in fantasy that they're not present in their physical body. They miss out on fully appreciating sensory experiences, such as enjoying a good meal. It's like only being half aware of it. Part of a Four's journey, if they experience this, is to get more in touch with being in their body.

Your Life Lesson and the Path of Integration: Everything is whole here and now. The feeling of longing, or that something's missing, holds you back from experiencing this wholeness. The lesson for Type 4s is to come to experience this wholeness. Over time, that feeling of longing will subside, replaced by a feeling of knowing that all is well.

Self-acceptance without having to meet a fantasized ideal is another lesson for Type 4s. You don't have to be the

3.4 TYPE 4 | 155

next Dostoyevsky, or Shakespeare, or Chopin, or whoever is the idol in your line of interest. Love your uniqueness and your own style, and accept yourself for who you *are*, without wasting your energy on becoming who you *want to be*.

Finally, being less identified with your emotions will help you to understand the real you. You are not your emotions — you may experience them quite strongly, but remember that they don't define you.

Daily Affirmations and Transformations for Type Fours:

- I NOW LET GO of my need to suffer
- I NOW ACCEPT that I should focus on fixing the reason behind my pain
- I NOW LET GO of feeling cast out and not worthy enough
- I NOW ACCEPT that I am important and should love myself for who I am
- I NOW LET GO of my need to procrastinate and always wait for the ideal moments
- I NOW ACCEPT that sometimes I will have to just act and perform, regardless of the timing
- I NOW LET GO of my need to be the most special person in the world
- I NOW ACCEPT that I am already leaving a unique mark

- I NOW LET GO of dwelling in the past
- I NOW ACCEPT that I should focus on the *right here, right now* more

COMPATIBILITY — HOW WELL "FOUR" SUITS THE OTHER TYPES

Type 1: I mentioned before that these types bring good balance to each other. However, Type 4s may eventually feel stifled by the rigidity of a Type 1. With that said, the stability they provide can be helpful for Type 4s, especially if the Type 1 is patient with their emotions.

Type 2: As I said, this can be a good combination. These two types can be emotionally available for each other in a deep and genuine way. The Two, being warm, considerate, and caring is comforting for a Type 4 during difficult times. If a Type 4 is acting in line with their stress line and the 2 is not in a good place, they may become overly dependent on each other.

Type 3: Type 4s may eventually find Type 3s to be too superficial, however, this combination can work out well. The Three helps the Four to be more practically focused. This can help with things like developing more structure and being action-oriented.

Type 4: Two Type 4s together can have a deep understanding of each other. They may develop deep bonds since they both understand the feelings of isolation they've experienced. This can lead to a very strong connection between them. They are not afraid to explore their shadows, and this can lead to a lot of spiritual and emotional growth. They can really help each other to heal emotionally and have a lot of respect for each other's emotions.

Type 5: Both types like to explore things in depth. They both have the capacity to be very creative, and you can be sure that some very interesting conversations will arise between them. The Four may find the Five creatively stimulating, and the Four helps the Five to stay in touch with their emotions.

Type 6: Sixes are also sensitive, hence, the depth of the relationship can have a similar quality to when two 4s are together. Sixes have more strength in their ability to cope, and so Fours can learn a lot from them. Sixes are loyal, which is another layer of support that Fours benefit from.

Type 7: Both these types have a sense of adventure, and Sevens can help Fours to have more new experiences. Fours often explore this adventure in their imagination while for Sevens, it's all about real experiences. They both seek newness, in different ways, and Sevens can bring fun, positivity, and resilience, helping Fours through difficult times.

Type 8: Both these types are intense, in different ways. They are both passionate and impulsive, however, this can sometimes lead to recklessness. Neither type likes to feel controlled, so any misunderstanding about one trying to control the other can lead to conflict.

Type 9: Both types are sensitive, but Nines bring a more calm and stable quality to the relationship. They respect each other's need for alone time but are emotionally available to each other. It's a comforting relationship for both but beware of the Nine's tendency to be a bit too withdrawn for the Four's liking at times.

MISIDENTIFICATION

Type 4s can be misidentified as Type 2s due to their emotional sensitivity. Another reason a Four could be misidentified as a Two is if they've had a particularly difficult time in their life, such as a depressive episode, especially if relationships are involved. They may look at this period of time and relate to the Two, so it's important to consider your long-term history. Ones can misidentify as a Four if they've been down or depressed lately. Sometimes, Nines are misidentified as Fours because they can also be very creative. However, the tell-tale sign is that Nines are a lot more even-tempered, without the emotional turbulence that Fours experience. Sixes are also misidentified as Fours, due to their sensitivity and feeling somewhat isolated and mistrustful of others.

AN OUTSIDER'S GUIDE TO TYPE 4S

To get along with me, understand that I might need a lot of time to myself. I have to process my emotions and it's not always easy to keep going as normal if I'm having a difficult time. I might seem unpredictable as well, and I can get hurt easily. It's helpful when people support me when I doubt myself.

To resolve conflict with me, give me space to express the way I feel. If you're too critical, I might feel like you're attacking me and I'll react badly. It's better if you show more empathy for my emotions and show understanding, then we can take it from there.

Type 5

The Alpha Geek

At their BEST:

cerebral
innovative
visionary
intellectual
knowledgeable
analytical
wise

At their WORST:

detached
isolated
overthinking
hoarder
stubborn
insecure
defensive

Shareable Quote:

I always think before I act;
I don't work well with feelings — I rely solely on facts.
Knowledge is my drug of choice;
I'd let you know how I feel if only I could find the voice.
I know I'm private, isolated, and sometimes aloof,
but I'm just pumping my intellect so I'll never be a goof.

3.5 TYPE 5

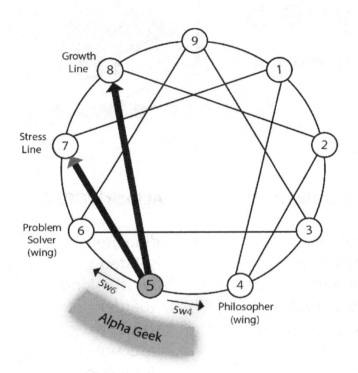

Enneagram Diagram for Type Five

Name: Type 5 — The Alpha Geek

AKA: The Specialist, The Investigative Thinker, The Scientist, The Innovator, The Expert

Personality: Five is probably that friend of yours who never seems to notice a pretty girl staring at him, or that

Brad-Pitt-like guy shooting her looks from across the bar. That happens because Five is usually lost deep within their thoughts, not because they're clueless. They probably invented the definition of *clue*.

Five is the kind of person you can talk to about anything. And I mean ANYTHING. From the latest global news and long-forgotten skills to weird sports like toe wrestling (look it up, it's a thing!). You can share your wildest dreams and *idée fixe* with them, and they'll have a lot to say about the matter. That's because *Five knows something about everything*. If you're attending a museum tour or bar trivia, Five's the guy you need by your side.

Fives are usually *loners*, meaning they don't jump into life feet first. They would rather stand from a safe distance and observe rather than pour their souls into active participation. That makes Fives seem emotionally distant, but they're not necessarily the black sheep in the group — they can be incredibly social, especially if they're among a knowledgeable crew.

If you're a Type 5, you're very intellectually curious, so much so that a day without learning feels like a dead day. You enjoy complex ideas, theories, and mental skills, and have an active imagination. You're insightful, and an independent and innovative thinker. You don't take anything at face value; rather, you want to explore it yourself. You study the way things work in depth, including life itself.

At your best, you're a pioneer. You're a visionary, able to see both reality and possibilities in ways that others just can't. You can create whole new worlds with your mind, and maybe even see these come into reality. At your worst, you can become extremely eccentric, meaning you have little point of reference for dealing with others. This can lead you to be a hermit and live in isolation. Also, because you cycle through so many ideas and beliefs, this can lead to nihilism and disillusionment, with you drawing the conclusion that participating in life is pointless.

Your Worst Fear: That you will not be able to take care of yourself. Ending up dependent on others scares the bejesus out of a Five because they believe that their secure independence is the core of living.

Your Heart's Desire: To truly understand every aspect of the world around you. Your motto is "knowledge means power," so seeking awareness and finding meaning in everything seems like the only way you can *live* in this world.

Your Biggest Sin: Hoarding feelings inside — while others seek love and comfort in relationships, you turn to gathering/sharing knowledge and information. Fives have difficulties opening up to their friends or partners emotionally. They often lean to self-disclosure, and so they skimp on their sentiments and hold back their affection from those who need it the most.

Wings:

5w4 The Philosopher — You delve into the difficult questions of life and want to get to the heart of issues. You're more emotional than other Fives, more independent, and self-absorbed. Feelings hit you hard, but more often than not, you find yourself not quite knowing how to process them. When in the middle of an emotional struggle, you'd rather be alone than in a group, and give your old pal melancholy a call.

Criticism stings you, people not understanding you both hurts and bores you, so you spend plenty of time alone. You get lost in a world of reading, fantasizing, and analyzing.

5w6 The Problem Solver — You're focused on intellectual pursuits, and you'd choose a lecture over a fun night with your friends/family in a heartbeat. You find social gatherings (and people, in general) to be energy-draining, but you are actually more social than 5w4. The emotional worlds of others seem both extremely boring and quite intimidating. You're not very sensitive yourself, either.

You turn your intellectual energy outward, learning about the world, acquiring skills that will help you conquer it. Fives with a 6 wing are a touch more anxious and fear-oriented, which makes them quite skeptical, especially of other people.

Subtypes:

Self-preservation Type 5 — The Castle Defender

You create a "castle" — a place where you can hide between the thick walls you've built to feel safe, but also so you can control what you know and are familiar with. Your castle may be your home, as in a physical place, or it may be in your mind. If it's in your home, you may be a hermit, a hoarder, or a prepper, happy to be spending time alone. If your castle is your mind, then you may never settle anywhere, always changing location and never creating any ties to any place or anyone.

The self-preservation Five is also a master for detachments — you don't open up freely, and you rarely ask for help. You know you're a self-preservation Five when you can listen to others for hours, always asking the right questions just so you can steer the conversation away to maintain a distance you're comfortable with. This type is the most hardcore Five you'll find, and it is unlikely to be mistaken with another Enneatype.

Social Type 5 — The Professor

You have a deep inner need to understand society, and you're driven by finding awareness, learning symbols, and in-depth analysis. You live your life in a constant pursuit of meaning and believe all things to be meaningless until you see the ultimate one. Unfortunately, your quest brings many sacrifices. You put every shred of energy into finding that knowledge and supreme sense that you eventually become uninterested in your everyday life.

These Fives rarely show their feelings and are pretty hard nuts to crack on an emotional level. They will hide behind their mask of intellect, believing that their knowledge makes them more valued and superior to others. They may have many friends, but those will be handpicked experts who share similar interests.

Sexual Type 5 — The Secret Agent (the countertype)

You cherish your independence but are also very drawn toward others. You carefully select your friends, people with whom you can share pieces of your rich inner world and knowledge. There is a push and pull between sharing and being secretive, as you don't trust people enough to give them all the information.

The secret agent is the countertype of Type 5, thanks to their ability to share their feelings with others. While the self-preservation and social Fives detach from their emotions, the sexual one is pretty sensitive and a die-hard romantic. Their final destination is reaching unconditional love, and they can become entirely transparent and intimate with the loved one, not holding anything back emotionally.

Stress Number: 7. When you're under stress and not feeling good, you become scattered and hyper. You bite off more than you can chew, cannot focus, feel impatient, and act impulsively. You step into the unhealthy side of Seven, where you get clingy of what you have just to make sure not to lose it. You can become a real hoarder when stressed, but piling things — whether physically or emotionally — just keeps shrinking the size of your world until you start feeling like you're suffocating.

Growth Number: 8. When you're in a good place you move toward the positive side of Eight, where you become self-confident and active in the world. You find it easier to make decisions, and you feel more at ease in various situations. Those around you will surely notice the difference because when feeling good, you get more energetic and actually quite chatty.

Center: You're in the Head, Thinking, or Fear Center. This mainly means that you're a thinker before a doer and that you turn to knowledge and information as your ticket to self-protection. You believe that you will not get harmed emotionally if you become *an expert* and know how to take advantage of any kind of situation. You embrace your center and externalize the main emotion — fear.

Famous 5s: Albert Einstein, Stephen Hawking, Buddha, Salvador Dali, Agatha Christie, Stephen King, Bill Gates, Sherlock Holmes, Albus Dumbledore (*Harry Potter*), Marie Curie, Al Pacino, Keanu Reeves, Dexter Morgan (*Dexter*), Fox Mulder (*The X-Files*).

Shareable Quote: *I always think before I act; I don't work well with feelings — I rely solely on facts. Knowledge is my drug of choice; I'd let you know how I feel if only I could find the voice. I know I'm private, isolated, and sometimes aloof, but I'm just pumping my intellect so I'll never be a goof.*

MY INNER WORLD

What I Like About Being this Type: Having an analytical mind is very empowering to me. I enjoy the fact that I can study things at length with extreme focus and have become an expert in several areas. I find it liberating to be knowledgeable enough to find solutions to complex problems, and that I can always approach my obstacles with a clear head and sharp mind. I enjoy that I am detail-oriented the real detective-style, which I achieve by being able to detach from feelings and observe objectively.

What's Hard About Being this Type: The practicalities of daily life can be really hard for me. I find it difficult to take care of myself physically. It certainly doesn't come naturally to me. I also dislike feeling fear and anxiety that I can't do things with such ease as others seem to do. I sometimes find it pretty nerve-racking to be in a larger group of people because I cannot seem to stay focused or energized the same way I am when I am in a more private company.

Your Personal Vices (addictions): You might take substances for mental stimulation or anxiety, but it's most likely that the way you abuse your body is by not taking care of it — poor eating, sleeping, and exercise habits.

Typical Thinking Patterns: You're constantly turning your attention outward to see how things work. Your mind is extremely active, finding patterns and connections and generating theories. As Sherlock Holmes said, your brain work is the only real thing to live for.

Typical Feeling Patterns: You often use mental stimulation and activity to divert your energy away from your feelings. When faced with a situation that you have to actively participate in, you may start feeling very anxious and fearful. You'd rather just detach and visit fantasy land instead.

SELF-DEVELOPMENT

When You're Very Healthy (levels 1 to 3): You can focus deeply and have razor-sharp powers of perception. You see things at a profound level, with insight and intelligence. You can see situations so clearly that you may even seem psychic in your ability to predict where they'll go next. You're an expert in several areas, and come up with original ideas in your field(s) of interest.

When You're Very Unhealthy (levels 7 to 9): When in a bad place, you're unstable and fearful of people and reality. You fixate on the threatening and dark side of human nature, and this horrifies and even tortures you. You withdraw from people, and may not even wish to live anymore. At your very worst, you could have a psychotic break or suffer from schizophrenia.

When You're Somewhere in Between (levels 4 to 6): You are truly intellectual and emotionally detached. You are either working on complicated ideas and plans in your mind or you're visiting your imaginary worlds. You reside in your *mind*, instead of in the *real world*. Your care for your physical needs is patchy, and you feel intense and irritable. Anyone who tries to remove you from your inner world gets very short shrift!

How to Maximize Your Potential: Find small ways to connect with both your body and the social world that you can keep going for the long-term. This will help you stay connected with physical reality. Aim for the phrase "head in the clouds, feet on the ground," which means you can still use your amazing power of visualization and original thought, but ground it in action and the real world by staying connected.

Red Flags to Watch Out for: Neglecting to take care of any of your physical needs. Going for days without having any meaningful social connection. Running away from any sort of conflict and spending hours going through ideas in your mind. You also might turn your attention off when around other people.

Self-Development Activities: Those that withdraw into themselves usually have a lot to work on so they can grow and thrive on a professional and emotional level. Fives are comfortable in their own minds and don't often feel like sharing or participating in the life that is going on around them. The most important self-development skill a Five should learn is to step out of their comfort zone and do things more actively.

Try Ditching the Knowledge — Telling a Five not to tap into their urge for learning is like telling a one-year-old not to touch the pacifier next to them. Okay, Five may not burst into tears, but they will surely feel like screaming inside. But, you don't necessarily need to *learn* something from every situation. Try muting your Five's personality, and do things just because. Go for a walk in the park without taking your book with you. When vacationing, just be on vacation — don't search for classes, museum tours, or opportunities to learn something new. Or at least, do that in smaller doses. Spend the rest of the time simply being there and relaxing.

Connect with Your Body — Fives retract into their minds and often disconnect from their bodies. Rediscovering this connection can be quite life-changing. Take up yoga or start exercising regularly. This will create a commitment to your health and body and force you to give yourself care that you otherwise wouldn't. It can also help you diffuse your intensity and nervousness — that way, you can use your high energy for your mental work, without it ending in melancholy, insomnia, or plain anxiety.

Stop Procrastinating — Sometimes, you can get into projects as a distraction or procrastination tool, and they actually don't serve your emotional or physical wellbeing or your progress in life. You will get much better results by taking action after some preparation, rather than dragging out the preparation process — you'd only be doing the latter out of fear. When working on a project, ask yourself whether your actions really support your goals or if you're doing it only to avoid doing something else. If it is the latter, stop, rewind, and readjust. Your emotional well-being will thank you later.

Allow Yourself Some Treats — Fives are minimalists at heart. They don't need too many things to feel good, but that can sometimes lean too heavily on the extreme side. You may need to have material security, but it is okay to treat yourself from time to time. Buy yourself a new dress, replace that squeaky couch with a new one, go on a trip — enjoy!

Doing Your Best in Relationships — Your bond with other people is an area you especially might feel anxious about. It feels very difficult to open up to people and trust them because of potential conflict and hurt down the line. But guess what? All Enneatypes go through conflicts, and all types can get hurt. The goal isn't to withdraw to avoid all that but to find a way to accept, learn, and overcome the issues.

- It is okay to be able to *hang out* without a particular reason or lesson to learn. Sometimes, you just have to show up for the people you love, even if you don't have anything to gain out of the situation.
- Take a risk and trust a friend — share some more of your life with other people, trusting they will keep the information to themselves.
- Stop hoarding your feelings — when a conflict arises, try to really feel those things rather than keeping them bottled up inside so you can process them later when you are on your own.
- Try to verbally share affirmation, appreciation, and your love with the people close to you. This may seem pointless to you, but some people just want to have somebody let them know they are appreciated.

Thriving at Work — Being a bottomless pit of knowledge, Five is usually the employee everyone wants to look up to. However, their desire to depend on predictability and their urge to hide behind their knowledgeable mask can cause them problems. To really thrive at work, Fives need to follow three golden rules:

3.5 TYPE 5 | 175

1. You don't have to know all of the answers. Making mistakes is human, so allow yourself a fair share of errors.
2. Share your thoughts even when you're unsure of yourself. Take the initiative, even if it ends up being not so right.
3. Participate more. You may hate meetings and gatherings, but being an active part of the team can throw many benefits your way.

Jobs and Career Paths: Many Type 5s might be engineers, scientists, mathematicians, computer programmers, or technicians, but this isn't always the case. There are also Fives that are authors, particularly of fantasy and sci-fi, where worldbuilding is a key element. A Type 5 might also be a scholar or work in any career that allows them to explore a field in depth and make original contributions.

The jobs that are the least attractive to Fives include bartender, waiter, retail worker, publicist, and pretty much every profession where people squeeze and drain your energy for things that are usually not your fault.

Activities and Hobbies: Perhaps the thing you enjoy more than anything else is research and learning. You will likely enjoy reading complex fiction and watching TV. Try to incorporate a physical hobby into your life, if you don't already have one.

SPIRITUALITY

Spiritual Struggles: Type 5s have a hard time believing the Universe or God will take care of them. You feel like the world is a dangerous place and that you have to make all the right steps to survive it. This involves hoarding knowledge, your emotional resources, your time, your privacy, and maybe your financial resources. Of course, all of these things can be positive. But when you are preparing and learning in a state of underlying terror, now that ends up being not so healthy.

Connecting with other people and yourself, and experiencing life physically, actually *living* instead of *observing*, is difficult for you. You've created a protective shield between yourself and the world with your mind. This protects you sometimes, but sometimes it only holds you back and prevents your progress.

When you think about Fives on a spiritual level, it is clear that they are advantageous, unlike the rest of the Enneatypes. They don't pump their egos, they are not so attracted to worldly things, need nothing more than simplicity, and can easily let go when the time comes. My cousin is a Five, and although she and her husband are clearly crazy for each other, I don't think she'll have a problem if the time for separation comes. He may be torn apart and devastated, but she will just press down the feelings, put on a brave face, and keep on going. This sounds like a strength, but it can hit her hard a bit too late. Fives need to learn how to *process* and *attach*, rather than *postpone* and *detach*.

Your life lesson and the path of integration: You can walk on the path of action and enjoy it. The feeling of fear of experience is what holds you back from experiencing true self-confidence and real-life progress. The more you take steps into reality, by trying, doing, deciding, and using your will, the less afraid you'll feel. It's not as bad as you think it's going to be.

Trust in the Universe or God, in its benevolence and *abundance*. Try to see the ways in which your action can be valuable, not just your knowledge. Shift your perspective away from believing you're someone unable to cope with life, into someone who uses their will, their head, their heart, and their gut to make decisions. Trust these decisions and stand by them. You're capable of making them. Many things will turn out in your favor. Those that don't? You've simply gained another learning experience, a *lived* learning experience. The realm of the abstract and the intellect can only give you part of this.

Daily Affirmations and Transformations for Type Fives:

- I NOW LET GO of frequently visiting my fantasy world

- I NOW ACCEPT that I should face reality more often
- I NOW LET GO of being afraid of the world around me
- I NOW ACCEPT that I might find beauty in uncertainties
- I NOW LET GO of isolating myself
- I NOW ACCEPT to spend more time with others
- I NOW LET GO of always looking for hidden motives in others
- I NOW ACCEPT that I should be more trusting
- I NOW LET GO of always looking for the reason and meaning of everything
- I NOW ACCEPT that it is okay to simply *be* and *feel*

COMPATIBILITY — HOW WELL "FIVE" SUITS THE OTHER TYPES

Type 1: You're both intelligent and have rich inner lives. You love to bounce ideas off each other and work together well in joint projects. The Type 1 can inspire you to put your knowledge into action, while you help them to be more adventurous in their thinking. But you can fall apart because Type 1s believe they have found objective truth, while you as a Type 5 don't believe in objective reality at all.

Type 2: A Type 2 will be fascinated by you because you're so distant and resistant to charm. They will help you take care of yourself physically, and you'll deeply appreciate this. You can be a good sounding board for an emotional Two, helping them to calm down and see things more logically. Type 2s can become overbearing, though, expecting you to give back as much as they give you, which you might not have the capacity for. They become more demanding, you withdraw more, and the relationship breaks down.

Type 3: You both work hard, and value expertise, excellence, and competency. You help them go deeper in their thinking, and they help you lighten up socially. They *sell* your skills to the outside world and can help you advance your career. You keep them steady on their path to success. However, you may compete with each other and neglect the emotional side of your relationship, which can lead to hostility.

Type 4: Both types like to explore things in depth. They can both be very creative, and you can be sure that some very interesting conversations will arise between them. The Four may find the Five to be creatively stimulating, and the Four helps the Five stay in touch with their emotions. However, a Five may see Four as too emotional, while a Four finds a Five not emotionally stimulating enough.

180 | NAKED WITH THE ENNEAGRAM

Type 5: This relationship usually moves slowly and with an overly respectful distance. Each finds the other intellectually stimulating and independent. They can become secretive, unwilling to share their lives with each other or make a real-world commitment, despite their depth of affection or feeling.

Type 6: You both have excellent intellectual skills and are great problem solvers, but the Six brings passion to the relationship, while the Five drags a soothing calm. This causes emotional tension because both types think in opposite ways, which can cause a standoff. A Six sees a Five as too conservative and driven by fear, and balks at the "strange" antisocial Five.

Type 7: Both these types love playing with ideas and debating, and can share a great sense of humor. A Seven can help a Five to become more in-tune with the world through fun and pleasurable experiences, while a Five can support a Seven to take themselves and life more seriously. The conflict usually comes from social styles — the Five thinks the Seven is too flowery, enthusiastic, and superficial. The Seven thinks the Five is far too serious and wants them to have more fun.

Type 8: Type 5 is a thinker, Type 8 is an action-taker, so you have a lot to learn from each other. You both love your independence and can have stimulating debates. The Eight will protect the Five, and the Five will advise the Eight. But in conflict, a Five resents an Eight for being too aggressive, and the Eight disrespects the Five for being weak. You get into a cycle of conflict and rejection.

Type 9: You give each other plenty of space, emotionally and physically. Nine respects the Five's intellect and curious mind, helping them "wake up" to reality. Nines can make Fives deeply relax and feel nurtured and safe. The danger is if both types are disconnected from themselves and living in fantasy. The relationship does not get off the ground or have enough stimulation to continue, because both parties are lost in their own minds and not truly living or being active in the world.

MISIDENTIFICATION

Type 5s are most likely to misidentify as Nines. They may also misidentify as Fours, especially if they have a dominant 4 wing. Both Fives and Nines frequently retreat into their minds and fantasies and don't take action in life, explaining the confusion between the types. But Type 9s are much softer and easy-going than Fives. They're more trusting and optimistic, too, and much less argumentative. A 5w4 or a 4w5? Well, Fours are more emotionally expressive and artistic than Type 5s. They are also more romantic and self-revealing, tending to seek closeness intensely, instead of close off from it and withdraw like a Five.

AN OUTSIDER'S GUIDE TO TYPE 5S

To get along with me, understand that I cherish my independence dearly. Don't try to make me conform to your expectations or the expectations of society — I'm a free thinker and an individual. In relationships, please don't be clingy, asking for too much of my time or energy. In terms of your expectations of me, make them clear, brief, and concise. If you come across as too emotional, I feel very uncomfortable and can't process what you're saying. I can find my affection for you most freely when I have a lot of time and space.

I might seem distant or arrogant at times, but that's usually because I'm feeling uncomfortable or trying to process my thoughts and emotions. I am not *cold;* I am just afraid of expressing and showing you my *warmth.*

Let's debate! I love throwing ideas around with like-minded people. But please, bring some knowledge to the table. Otherwise, I will find you boring and will quickly retreat to my inner worlds.

Type 6

The Eternal Worrier

At their BEST:

loyal
responsible
committed
nonconformist
prepared
trustworthy
friendly

At their WORST:

anxious
paranoid
hypervigilant
indecisive
pessimistic
fearful
confrontative

Shareable Quote:

I am anxious, skeptical, and I worry a lot,
but I'm here to stay and be the most loyal friend you've got.
No adventure can turn into a misadventure when I'm in charge,
I have a backup plan and few alternatives,
so we're well covered by and large.
I am sometimes afraid and get insecure,
so I rely on you, my friend, to be my warmth and cure.

3.6 TYPE 6

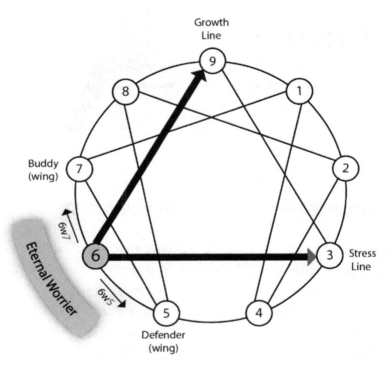

Enneagram Diagram for Type Six

Name: Type 6 — The Eternal Worrier

AKA: The Loyal Skeptic, The Guardian, The Doubter, The Security Seeker, The Questioner

Personality: Six is probably your friend who has been stuck in their miserable job or unfulfilling relationship because they are too scared to make a change. But don't mistake Six for a wuss; they are just 24/7 worriers. They fear making a change because of the unpredictability that transitions bring. They are anxious by nature, always concerned about how things can get worse. This can be mild, like bringing an extra sweater *just in case*, or more extreme like stockpiling their storm shelter so they can be prepared for the possible apocalypse (Doomsday could be any day, people!).

Six is a friend for life. They are the type of people that you hang out with since kindergarten and share most of your life with. I have a Six in my life, and even though we live countries apart, she regularly calls to just *check in*, and make sure I am safe. Although her constant worrying, like please-don't-eat-popcorn-while-talking-you-might-choke-to-death, can sometimes get annoying, her loyalty and care are why I love her so dearly.

If you're a Type 6, you're very oriented to security and stability. But how this manifests depends on if you're phobic or counterphobic, two different types of Sixes. You might show one of these styles all the time, or more likely, you switch between the two. Both types are extremely anxious and fearful and are fueled by stress and worry. When in a phobic state, you are cautious, suspicious, and indecisive.

And I mean really indecisive. You are the type of person who looks at a pair of jeans and spends the next hour checking other options, just to end up buying the first one you laid your eyes on. You may have lost an hour, but hey, at least you're sure that your bottom doesn't look better in another pair.

You don't like thinking about huge commitments. You're likely to search for comfort and security in everything, and seek out authority to obey.

In a counterphobic state, you see danger and provoke it, acting tough and aggressive. If phobic Six craves security, the counterphobic one craves the exact opposite — insecurity. They see danger lurking in every corner and they feel the need to attack. For instance, if you see a Six going through a very challenging time of their life without breaking down, know that their counterphobic nature has already been prepared for the strike. In fact, they have probably gone through that scenario a dozen times. Which is why they seem like they have everything under control. Counterphobic Six does what they fear!

At your best, you are self-reliant and a champion for yourself and others. At your worst, you can get yourself in dangerous situations (counterphobic) or become a shell of yourself, dependent on an external authority (phobic) for your identity and safety. You can overidentify and idealize authority, leading to harmful behaviors and persecuting others, not in the select group.

Your Worst Fear: That you will lose your stability. Six is terrified of unpredictable outcomes that they have not been prepared for, in a ready-for-the-worst-but-hoping-for-the-best kind of way. They feel comfortable when everything is *just as is,* even if they are not actually satisfied with *as is.* They would rather be a little miserable than have to change things and risk spoiling what they already have.

Your Heart's Desire: To feel secure and safe. The Eternal Worrier seeks this kind of support as compensation for their unconditional loyalty to others, forming strong bonds and stable relationships that they can count on.

Your Biggest Sin: Extreme preparing for the future. Six is a person who plans well-ahead for unfortunate events. In the case of an outbreak, Six will probably be the only type who has things figured out. They will be like, "Grab that red bag from the back of the closet, put this gas mask on, and let's go!"

Wings:

6w5 The Defender — You want to stand up for the underdog, but also gravitate toward authority rather than being a rebel. You have an intellectual streak and are self-controlled and moral. You prefer to be right and to make progress than to be liked. The defender's coping mechanism is projecting their feelings onto other people.

The Five wing here helps Six find solutions to their problems rather than get tangled in all of their anxious feelings. However, just like a Five, this type of Six is also prone to withdrawing into their mind and experiencing trouble expressing their emotions.

The defender is also prone to suffering from *analysis paralysis* because of their inability to process things in a healthy and timely manner.

6w7 The Buddy — You're playful and relaxed, seeking fun, enjoyment, and social experiences, especially spontaneously. You're more of a free spirit than pure 6 or 6w5, and dislike planning or looking too far into the future. Generally, you are easy to get along with and build a large social network in the form of "insurance."

You may be more laid back, but The Buddy is still a Six, meaning you don't separate from your worrying completely. You still find backup plans and having extra reinforcements essential when making preparations.

Subtypes:

Self-preservation Type 6 — The Family Loyalist

You're focused on family, whether that's your actual biological family or a created "family" of friends. You craft safety by finding allies, using your warmth and charm to appeal to them. You fear insecurity the most, which is why you create close relationships — you need to feel comfortable and safe around people you can trust.

The self-preservation Six is the most phobic of all Sixes and is torn between how they perceive the world internally and externally. On the inside, this Six is afraid, insecure, and feels tormented, while their external reality is peaceful and warm. The family loyalist tries to compensate for the inner anguish by seeking protection and security in external sources or through forming friendships and alliances with other people.

Social Type 6 — The Social Guardian

You see yourself as a preserver of the social order, and you take this as your duty. You protect a group and its policies, including chastising those who break order. You could be subservient to a leader, or you could rebel against them if they go against the rules.

You lack trust, either in yourself or other people, and try to rely on *authorities* so you can find your security in reason and rules. Compared to the self-preservation type, the social Six has a stronger personality in terms of certainty. The social guardian is not insecure, but in an attempt to avoid being uncertain, they can become *too sure* of things. In more extreme cases, this Six can become a fanatic.

You need to have a clear system to trust and follow so that everything in the world can make sense. At times, this subtype of Six can be mistaken for a One, thanks to their controlling, self-critical, and demanding nature.

Sexual Type 6 — The Warrior (the countertype)

Your main goal is to have an impact. You want to develop your own strength, finding safety either in your physical strength or in various ideas and philosophies. You may also seek to create beauty in the outer world as a form of security.

The sexual Six is the countertype of this Enneatype because they step away from the constant fear and put on an offensive mask, becoming ready for being attacked. As the name suggests, the warrior seems bold, fierce, and with an aggressive attitude toward danger. However, even though the sexual Six gives the impression that they are fearless, they can become paranoid of those around them, believing that anyone, at any time, can become a possible threat to them.

Stress Number: 3. When you're under stress and not feeling good, you become very arrogant and start showing the worst sides of the Three. You don't mind stepping on anyone for success, demonizing those outside your inner circle, and becoming ferociously competitive against people you are not comfortable with. Just like a Three, when stressed, Six hides their anxiety by presenting themselves as someone who has it all figured out. This contradicts their lack-of-confidence personality, which only shoves them deeper into stress.

Growth Number: 9. When you're in a good place, you become much more relaxed and easygoing, like a healthy Type 9. You're able to understand different points of view and accept more people rather than just your chosen group. You don't obsess about potential threats as much, and you pause on preparing and planning for unfortunate situations, so you can simply *be in the moment.* When feeling secure, Six may actually start feeling like things will turn out to be just fine.

Center: You're in the Head, Thinking, or Fear Center. You don't act impulsively but plan well before taking a step. The main emotion that dictates your actions is fear, so you are mostly focused on managing the perceived dangers of life and making sure you are secure by forming alliances for protection. In other words, you are out of touch with your center and its core emotion.

Famous 6s: Ellen DeGeneres, Robert F. Kennedy, Marilyn Monroe, Richard Nixon, Malcolm X, Sigmund Freud, Robert De Niro, Mel Gibson, Julia Roberts, Jennifer Aniston, Frodo Baggins (*Lord of the Rings*), Adolf Hitler, Chuck Norris, Prince Harry.

Shareable Quote: *I am anxious, skeptical, and I worry a lot, but I'm here to stay and be the most loyal friend you've got. No adventure can turn into a misadventure when I'm in charge, I have a backup plan and a few alternatives, so we're well covered by and large. I am sometimes afraid and get insecure, so I rely on you, my friend, to be my warmth and cure.*

MY INNER WORLD

What I Like About Being this Type: I like being committed to my family and friends, and being someone they can depend on. I love that I can be a valued member of a group and safeguard and protect the group and its principles. I enjoy being steadfast and reliable.

What's Hard About Being this Type: The uncertainty, fear, and worry of being a Type 6 get to me. I worry about people taking advantage of me and wear myself out looking for danger. I also wish I didn't overthink things to the point of being suspicious and doubting others and myself.

Your Personal Vices (addictions): You might use caffeine to keep your energy stable. When you're anxious, you might reach for alcohol or other depressants to help you cope. Gulping a few shots may also become a crutch to help you relax and quiet your mind.

Typical Thinking Patterns: You're constantly turning your attention to danger. You are very likely to evaluate everything you come across in terms of safety. If you're counterphobic (like the sexual subtype), you will forge ahead with the most dangerous option, while if you're phobic, you will focus on surrounding yourself with people as a form of security.

Typical Feeling Patterns: Most of your emotions convert into fear and worry — fear of being alone, being abandoned, and being without support. The thing that makes you the most anxious is being without protection, so you place all of your energy into building one so you will finally feel safe.

SELF-DEVELOPMENT

When You're Very Healthy (levels 1 to 3): You're lovable, warm, appealing, affectionate, and funny. You place a high value on trust, and you make time to bond with others. You're independent and interdependent. You have a true belief in yourself and feel courageous and brave to champion others, as well. You can be an excellent leader.

When You're Very Unhealthy (levels 7 to 9): You feel like everyone is out to get you, and you perceive the world as a dangerous place. You become volatile and desperate, believing you're not good enough to be included. You feel defenseless in the face of the world. You criticize others and disparage them, and can also become passive-aggressive. You may start to rely on alcohol, drugs, or turn violent, just so you can press the "mute" button on your anxieties.

When You're Somewhere in Between (levels 4 to 6): You're vigilant, watching out for problems that may threaten your stability. You're passive-aggressive under stress and feel indecisive and cautious. You are confused within, so give mixed signals to others. You become insular with your social circle, disliking outsiders, and watching out for enemies and threats.

How to Maximize Your Potential: Breathe through your anxiety. Notice it as it is happening, before reacting. Sit with your stress, and try to reflect. Remember, many things you have been terrified of did not happen at all. Plus, by keeping an optimistic attitude, you can *create* positive outcomes. You have more power than you realize. Life is not just happening *to* you; you can take an active role for the best by being positive and guarding against catastrophic thoughts.

Red Flags to Watch Out for: Being snappy and irritable — this means you're not working with your anxiety, you're being led by it. Blaming others for bad things that happen — sometimes things just happen, and sometimes you've brought it on yourself. Being very critical to people outside your chosen "group" can also be a negative personality trait to look out for.

Self-Development Activities: Think of the mind of Six to be a covered pot filled with water and placed over high heat. At first, it starts to get warm — which can be Six realizing the dangers of the world. But then, as Six thinks more about the potential consequences, the water gets hotter and hotter, until it finally reaches a boiling point. But Six is not done yet. They actually let their emotions bubble inside, replaying self-created negative scenarios in their heads, which only makes them more and more anxious. The bubbles now push the steam up, forcing the lid to dance on top of the pot, getting ready for the inevitable spillage. To avoid making a huge mess on the stove, and to stop Six from crumbling under the pressure of stress and anxiety, they need to find activities that will reduce the heat, half-open the lid and let the steam escape.

Meditate — Although everyone can benefit from regular meditation practice, Six is way past *can benefit*. To them, this calming act of getting yourself together is essential. So, if you are a Six, try to find a decent practice that will calm your ever-worrying mind. But you don't have to turn to Buddhism to benefit from meditation. You don't even have to be spiritual. You can simply start being more mindful. Sit down, close your eyes, and spend the next 15 minutes focusing on your senses. What can you hear? How does the sensation on your skin feel? Focus on the silence, on the emptiness of having your eyes closed. Whatever keeps you away from your thoughts, do it!

Breathe it Out — We've already mentioned this, but it would be remiss not to make it an activity. Whenever you feel your thoughts become a bit too much for your fragile mind, *stop*. Don't let your anxiety take over, but release it through your breaths. Whenever feeling stressed, just take a deep breath. Inhale deeply, keep the breath there for one, two, three, then release slowly through your nose. And do it again. And again. And yet again. Breathe in, focus on the emotion, then imagine it leaving your body as the air leaves your nostrils.

Avoid Negative Things — Whatever feeds your pessimistic outlook, avoid it. My Six friend stopped watching the news a long time ago because whenever she would hear a negative story, her anxiety meter would start beeping, and she would feel like all hope was lost. *Where is this world headed to?* If you, too, cannot handle such things, avoid anxious reinforcement whenever you can. Customize your TV exposure, and become more selective about the things you read, hear, and see.

Find a Centering Prayer and Stick to It — Again, you don't need to be spiritual or religious for this, but repeating motivating words to yourself can seriously enhance your mood and improve your outlook. Whether something like "I am strong, and I will be alright," or "The sun still shines after heavy storms," find your boosting mantra and stick to it.

Doing Your Best in Relationships — Six is not really the easiest person to have around. They are way too worried about the future and potential negative outcomes that they are willing to drag their partner/friend into their fearful and anxious whirlwind along with them. Also, their insecurities and questions like, "Do you still love me?" or, "Am I really your best friend?" can wreak havoc on their bond with other people. To stop yourself from being too much of a Six, you need to be mindful about your actions toward others:

- Stop seeing everyone you meet as a threat — the world is not really out to get you, so whenever such thoughts pop up, say "I should give this person a chance," to yourself.
- Learn to accept compliments — not everyone has unhealthy motivations behind positive words.
- Cut back on sharing your negative perceptions with your partner. Whenever you catch yourself trying to nag them about things like not screwing the bolts of the cabinets more securely, bite your tongue, and try to be more realistic. What are the chances of the cabinet door actually killing you during an earthquake?
- Stop being so suspicious. Go back to the earlier days of your relationships, and replay some good memories. Do you still believe that your partner/friend doesn't want you around anymore?

Thriving at Work — At work, Sixes are real troubleshooters. That means that they thrive when the bar is not so high because they love to be the ones finding the solution. They would rather wait and think things through instead of acting recklessly, which makes them the perfect employees. However, they still have three golden rules to follow to become the best versions of themselves:

1. Watch out for your unhealthy connection with authority. You can either be following it blindly or having an unmerited rebellious tendency. Become more conscious, instead.
2. Don't always be the one to point the flaws in projects you haven't worked on.
3. Keep your self-confidence in check — keep a journal of all your professional achievements, regardless of how minor, and remind yourself regularly that you are a needed member of the team.

Jobs and Career Paths: You can thrive in a long-term role with an organization where you feel valued and have a sense of purpose. You can work very well in a team. You will want a role with clear expectations and where you can show your loyalty, either to your team, your customers, or the people you help, if you work for a charity.

Your dream job should be able to turn worrying into something positive. Think teachers, analysts, writers, activists, etc. The job you wouldn't be satisfied with is the one that includes risk. Think investment bankers, for instance.

Activities and Hobbies: It's likely that you'll volunteer and be part of lots of groups and societies. You enjoy having a personal space that is all your own where you can read, write, play music, and do something creative.

SPIRITUALITY

Spiritual Struggles: Type 6s have a hard time believing that God and the Universe will take care of them, but also that they can be their own sense of security. While it's good to have a support network and financial stability to fall back on in times of trouble, even if you *do* have these, it is likely that you're still wracked with anxiety. You never feel safe or secure enough.

This means that you may be spiritually "warm," rather than hot or cold. You probably have an affinity toward spirituality because you like to be protected by an authority figure, i.e., God or the Universe. However, you don't feel enough trust for this authority that you allow yourself to completely follow it. Instead, you're always hedging your bets with other sources of security. You may find that you become very loyal to a church or particular religious figure, which can both help and harm your spiritual journey. It can help because you can learn a lot, but it can harm you because you may spiritually outgrow the organization or mentor, but find it very hard to move on. You may find that it's actually the community *surrounding* the spirituality that you draw comfort and security from, rather than the divine itself. This can be a pitfall.

Your Life Lesson and the Path of Integration: Your path of integration is getting to know that your deepest sense of security comes from *within*. On the spiritual path, your goal is to get to a point of relaxation, of surrender, even, where you trust yourself and God/the Universe/life itself, to take care of you. You feel support from your own heart, and you know how to take care of yourself emotionally.

Another lesson to learn is the power of thoughts and imagination. Your thoughts are often anxious and negative, imagining unsafe scenarios. You dwell in a place of fear. As many great minds have said over centuries, "Fear is faith in reverse." Faith is a very powerful energy and mind-space to be in. It energizes us and helps us achieve more than we would ever otherwise. It gives us courage and strength. So as you can imagine, fear does the opposite — draining us and weakening us. Experiment with a mindset of faith, even in small scenarios. Notice how different you feel — lighter, freer, and more relaxed. Also, notice if you start getting more positive outcomes and results due to having a faith-based mindset.

Daily Affirmations and Transformations for Type Sixes:

- I NOW LET GO of my fear of being alone in the world
- I NOW ACCEPT that I am an independent person and can take care of myself

- I NOW LET GO of my never-ending fear of the future
- I NOW ACCEPT that I should focus more on the positive side of things
- I NOW LET GO of always being suspicious of other people
- I NOW ACCEPT that you cannot really *know* someone unless you let them in
- I NOW LET GO of overthinking and exaggerating my problems
- I NOW ACCEPT that I should be more confident about the challenges I face
- I NOW LET GO of my need to look for my security in other people
- I NOW ACCEPT that I am capable of providing and protecting myself, regardless of the situation

COMPATIBILITY — HOW WELL "SIX" SUITS THE OTHER TYPES

Type 1: Sixes and Ones have a lot in common with their approach, so they make a good combination and have a strong foundation of loyalty in their relationship. At the core, Six can seem warmer, as they are not likely to lash out in anger as often as One. One would probably *wear the pants* in this relationship and have the final word. If One becomes too judging and critical, Six can go deeper into their anxiety and insecurity, which will probably be the crack of this relationship.

Type 2: A relationship between a Type 2 and Six has a foundation of trust and dependability. They both treat their commitment to each other as very important. Twos should be mindful that Sixes can perceive unwanted advice as intrusive and undermining their confidence. If a Six wants your help, they will make it known.

Type 3: Both types are action-oriented, hard workers. Type 6s have a compassionate quality about them. They may help Type 3s that have more superficial tendencies to focus more on others, such as those that are in need.

Type 4: Sixes are also sensitive, hence, the depth of the relationship can have a similar quality to when two Fours are together. Sixes have more strength in their ability to cope, and so Fours can learn a lot from them. Sixes are loyal, which is another layer of support that Fours benefit from.

Type 5: You both have excellent intellectual skills and are great problem solvers, but the Six brings passion to the relationship, while the Five brings a soothing calm. But this causes emotional tension and you think in opposite ways, which can cause a standoff. A Six sees a Five as too conservative and driven by fear, while a Six balks at the "strange" antisocial Five.

Type 6: You bond very well with another Six, and can have a fun, playful relationship with a lot of shared values and activities. You can trust each other deeply and confide in each other in a way you couldn't do with other types. However, if one of you takes a bad emotional turn, it's likely the other will be deeply affected and you'll feed off each other.

Type 7: This is a great pair, full of witty banter, jokes, and fun. Type 7s come up with great ideas, while Sixes have the organizational skills to follow them through. Sevens lift the spirits of a Type 6 and open them to experiences and opportunities. But when they're unhealthy, Sevens seem irresponsible and a weak foundation for security-seeking Sixes, while Sevens feel the Sixes hold them back and are too negative.

Type 8: Both types are suspicious of the world and other people. Type 8s take care of their own interests, while Sixes build a network. When they get through each other's walls, they have a deep bond of trust. Epic power struggles can be a problem, with either an aggressive counterphobic Six or a passive-aggressive Six.

Type 9: Sixes and Nines can get along very well. They both want stability and peace of mind. They usually fall into line with normal societal values, and the counter-phobic Six can match the counter-cultural streak of the Nine. The two types, however, do not share their feelings, and this can lead to problems festering and not being addressed. This can lead to explosive rage on behalf of the Six, and withdrawal or matched rage on behalf of the Nine.

MISIDENTIFICATION

Type 6s are often misidentified as Type 2s. Both are warm and sociable, with a large social network. The key difference is that Twos want more intimacy and want to nurture and take care of pretty much anyone, while Sixes are much more discerning and slow to trust, and don't see the relationship as a nurturing one. Sixes may also mistype as Fives, because they're both very intellectual. However, Sixes are more linear and traditional in their thinking, while Fives are wilder and more experimental.

AN OUTSIDER'S GUIDE TO TYPE 6S

I want you to hear my anxieties, without judging me for them. I know I overreact, but try not to take it too seriously. Just listen to me and work things through with me, and I'll be fine. My immediate reaction is fear, but I can also be brave and strong.

I love making jokes and laughing with you — it's my favorite form of bonding. Let me know that everything is okay with us, as I tend to worry about where the relationship is going and if you feel as strongly as I do. I have a fear of being abandoned, so please don't cut me off if I've done something wrong. Instead, address it with me.

I do like to have new experiences, but I can be scared of them at first. Gently push me, and I'll have a ton of fun with you!

Type 7

The Fun Lover

At their BEST:

fun
energetic
free-spirited
optimistic
spontaneous
lively
adventurous

At their WORST:

distractible
scattered
directionless
impulsive
restless
undisciplined
irresponsible

Shareable Quote:

I am chatty, fun, and make friends on the go;
join me on my adventures and pleasure I will show.
I run away from the boring, dull, and all things ordinary —
come with me now,
and see what it means to be merry.
I get afraid too, even though I will not let you know,
but if you're up for a new experience,
I'll be as happy as a kid when it snows.

3.7 TYPE 7

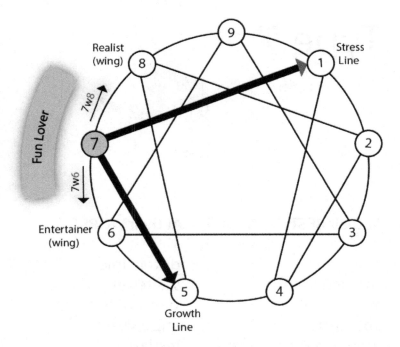

Enneagram Diagram for Type Seven

Name: Type 7 — The Fun Lover

AKA: The Adventurer, The Entertaining Optimist, The Pleasure-Seeker, The Positive Planner, The Enthusiast

Personality: Seven is that person who is always on the go. You know, that 40-something-dude who has more youthful energy than his 17-year-old kid. The one who is always first to jump into last-minute experiences. The guy you need to bump into at a boring dinner party so you can spend the rest of the evening doing something actually fun. That guy! My guy!

Yes, my partner is a Seven, and God do I envy his laid-back, never-ending lust for life. Several years of living together, one dog, and countless fights like *put-a-darn-coaster-under-your-beer* later, I finally throw my hands up and admit it — I wish we could swap personalities. But don't tell him I said that!

Seven is also the kind of person that makes friends wherever they go, and always has cracking stories to share. And I'm talking about waking-up-on-a-yacht-owned-by-Madonna type of stories.

When they are at their healthiest, I guess Seven is my favorite number on the Enneagram. But I know that all is not peachy even in Seventh Heaven. Wipe their vividness off, and you will see that fear of pain creeps from underneath.

If you're a Type 7, you love stimulation and keeping yourself busy. You probably have six projects on the go at one time! You love to have new and exciting experiences and have spontaneous fun. You're an optimist, a jack-of-all-trades, and a true extrovert. You love conversations, debates, and learning new things by actually experiencing them.

At your best, you slow down a bit, focus your talents on goals that really matter to you, and experience real inner joy, not just temporary thrills. At your worst, you're scattered and undisciplined and have a bunch of ideas or short-term experiences that don't amount to anything long-term.

Your Worst Fear: That you're missing out on new experiences. The biggest fear of a Seven is living a dull and boring, 9-to-5, sometimes-free-on-the-weekend kind of life.

Your Heart's Desire: To feel truly and deeply contented and satisfied without any ties.

Your Biggest Sin: Fear of commitment. Seven is the type of girl who runs away from the altar and spends her entire life regretting not marrying the love of her life. She may not show it, but she will be hurting deeply inside.

Wings:

7w6 The Entertainer — You have amazing people skills, with stories to tell and anecdotes to share, and are very oriented to making connections with others. You care for others but keep your independence. You're more organized and committed than the pure Seven, but tend to find conflict extremely awkward.

Just like a Six, you are very loyal to your friends and family, feeling a strong duty to stick by the ones you love.

You may want new experiences, but you will never bounce around endlessly. You need to finish the project you are working on first, before being ready to move on to the next thing.

7w8 The Realist — You have so many commitments and activities going on, you find it hard to tend to your relationships. Your *my way or the highway* type of thinking forces you to prioritize your own needs over those of others, but that doesn't apply to the people close to you. You find the happiness of your partner/friends/family pretty important.

You want freedom, control, experiences, and luxury, and are strong-willed enough to get them all. This can make you competitive and aggressive, but thanks to your persuasiveness, you actually seem to get things your way.

Subtypes:

Self-preservation Type 7 — The Gourmand

You're focused on the good life for you and your family. Great meals, parties, business deals to provide as much as possible, laughter, expensive vacations — you love it all. You need The American Dream to be happy. The self-preservation Seven is the definition of a *playboy* or a *playgirl*. They're talkative, cheerful, and warm, but their greed for all things pleasurable can be spotted from miles away.

This subtype is great at forming *networks* or friendship alliances that put them in a privileged position. They can be judgmental or dismissive of those outside their family circle, whether biological or surrogate. They are usually not philanthropic or charitable, but opportunistic, self-oriented, and pragmatically calculating.

Social Type 7 — The Social Visionary (the countertype)

You want to achieve a rank in a particular community, which gives you more self-discipline and follow-through. You're able to sacrifice your personal preferences but may become bored with this if it does not bear fruit quickly. You can be an entrepreneur with your numerous ideas, but you need a solid team to establish the structures required to make a business work.

As the countertype, the social Seven wants to be pure and good rather than do things out of greed. The social visionary is not that focused on taking advantage of opportunities; they often postpone their own needs to focus on serving others.

Sexual Type 7 — The Adventurer

You're fascinated by people, ideas, and places. You have great sales skills and are a fantastic talker, but you can also be gullible. You're full of the possibilities of life and plan to experience as many as possible, but you can lose your sense of purpose while exploring these.

You are a die-hard dreamer, always imagining things in a better light than what reality casts. You know that feeling you have right after falling in love? Well, that is how the adventurer sees the world all the time — with passion and lust.

Their fantasy-driven thoughts and actions can sometimes be just a distraction to avoid some painful part of their life.

Stress Number: 1. When you're under stress and not feeling good, you become very judgmental, critical, and rigid in your thinking, showing the worst sides of the One. You become perfectionistic and paralyzed by self-judgment. You talk down about others' choices and moral fiber. The stressed Seven often takes their rose-colored glasses off and starts seeing the world as black and white only.

Growth Number: 5. When you're in a good place, you become much more focused, and you begin to go into depth in areas that interest you, rather than thinking you're missing out and skimming the surface of everything. By taking on the traits of a Five, you are no longer as focused on *getting,* and actually start *giving.* Secure Sevens are capable of recognizing their fears and find satisfaction not in the fantasy, but in the realness of the world.

Center: You're in the Head, Thinking, or Fear Center. Just like with Five and Six, Seven's deepest emotion is also fear. But unlike Five and Six, Seven actually hides from their fear. They use their outgoing personality to shush their fear of getting hurt and often distract themselves with all sorts of pleasures to avoid the pain. By avoiding your center, you avoid the fear and keep these emotions tightly pressed inside.

Famous 7s: Mozart, John F. Kennedy, Britney Spears, Brad Pitt, Meghan Markle, Elton John, Fergie, Steven Spielberg, Cher, Tina Turner, George Clooney, Robin Williams, Bruce Willis, Cameron Diaz, Peter Pan, Catherine Zeta-Jones, Steve Jobs, Jeff Bezos, Leonardo da Vinci, Eddie Murphy, Leonardo DiCaprio.

Shareable Quote: *I am chatty, fun, and make friends on the go; join me on my adventures and pleasure I will show. I run away from the boring, dull, and all things ordinary — come with me now, and see what it means to be merry. I get afraid too, even though I will not let you know, but if you're up for a new experience, I'll be as happy as a kid when it snows.*

MY INNER WORLD

What I Like About Being this Type: I love my optimistic outlook and my free-spirited nature. I like being outrageous, larger-than-life, and outspoken. It's fun! I like that

I'm brave and bold enough to have exciting adventures and unique experiences.

What's Hard About Being this Type: I wish I had more time to do more things, and the discipline to see things through to the end. I wish I could feel more comfortable in commitment — to a career or a relationship — but I always seem to feel like I'm missing out.

Your Personal Vices (addictions): This type is prone to addictions of many different types because they want to escape mundanity and always be on a "high." When Seven is unable to go on adventures or try out new things for some reason, they often turn to drugs or alcohol as a way to get away from the boring reality.

Typical Thinking Patterns: You're always thinking about options. Are there more options, better options, exciting options? The world is truly your oyster, and you gravitate toward the new, the exciting, the luxurious, and the pleasurable.

Typical Feeling Patterns: You're extremely excitable and feel enthusiastic a lot of the time. Without a constructive outlet for your energy, you feel scattered, hyper, and even manic. You may also always feel a longing, a desire to move, to shift, to get out, a yearning for something new and fresh.

SELF-DEVELOPMENT

When You're Very Healthy (levels 1 to 3): You're enthusiastic, talented, adaptable, and responsive. You love life and all it has to offer and enjoy making connections with people. You feel cheerful, resilient, and optimistic. You deeply appreciate all the experiences you have, which makes you feel appreciative and grateful. You're awed by the world, by the simple things in life, and have positive, expansive thoughts and emotions.

When You're Very Unhealthy (levels 7 to 9): You feel very anxious and restless. You channel your energy into pleasure and more pleasure and struggle to get anything done. You become abusive and offensive, acting impulsively and irresponsibly. You have wild mood swings and feel claustrophobic and panic-stricken one moment, excited the next. In a really bad place, you can give up on life altogether.

When You're Somewhere in Between (levels 4 to 6): You're adventurous, with a ton of ideas, but not very focused. You love the latest trends and keeping up with them. You have far too much going on and can't keep up with commitments. You start to "perform," telling wild stories, exaggerating, and telling constant jokes.

How to Maximize Your Potential: You have so many ideas and urges that they scatter your energy and leave you without direction if you follow them all. To grow, you need to start discerning between your better ideas and impulses, and the ones that will get you nowhere.

Red Flags to Watch Out for: Becoming irresponsible and looking for instant pleasures to get you through the day. When not in a healthy place, Seven can become reckless, and in order to avoid pain, they can even risk more than they can afford to lose just so they feel good again.

Self-Development Activities: Seven oozes optimism and sprite energy, but that doesn't mean that everything is as peachy inside. Although the most cheerful of all, this Enneatype still has many issues to resolve to become the best version of themselves. And trust me, when Seven is truly healthy, the world really does seem to be a better place. Even for those who are with them. But first, some self-development activities are in order.

Practicing Gratitude — Seven is so busy looking for the *next* great thing that they overlook what great things they already have and have experienced. I'm sure you already have a journal for your ideas. Why not start a gratitude journal? Each morning, think of three things you're grateful for, or each night, write down three things that happened in the day that make you feel thankful. Notice the small things, the little moments of sunshine in your day. This will help you stay focused and committed to your existing projects and commitments.

Becoming Self-Disciplined — This may sound like a harsh or austere thing, but it doesn't have to be. Often you ride the buzz of a new idea, relationship, or project, but then get disillusioned when things get hard. This prevents you from making progress. But here's the thing — if you choose something or someone that really means something to you, you can improve self-discipline by *choosing* to find the new, the beautiful, the exciting, *within* that thing, every day. This will help you focus your attention on your commitment and help you progress without feeling depressed or like you're missing out. Choose to keep your eyes focused on one thing, rather than getting distracted by the periphery.

Become More Moderate — Although restraint is not really in Seven's dictionary, it is a term that is more than worth exploring — it is essential. Seven always seems to jump head-first whenever a new opportunity comes their way, which is as risky and reckless as it is courageous. Try to be moderate about the things you are doing and stick to the golden middle. Pass on a fun night out if you've already spent the previous two nights on crazy adventures.

Exercise Daily — Regular exercise is important for everyone, but for a bottomless pit of energy like Seven, it is actually crucial. Burning off excess energy and calming your high-strung spirit will help you to be able to put your focus on less-exciting things, as well.

Doing Your Best in Relationships — Being with a Seven means you are in for excitement, spontaneous decisions, and a forever-young lifestyle. There will never be a boring moment when Seven is by your side, regardless of how dull the situation may be. Their optimism has an almost infectious bite, and once you let a Seven in, their enthusiasm will win you for life. But that doesn't mean that Seven doesn't have some improving to do relationship-wise:

- Sometimes you just have to *be there* without looking for excitement or turning the situation into something that it's not. Your partner/friend will sometimes need you to just bring your listening ear.
- Don't always try to cheer someone up. When your partner/friend is going through a tough time, you need to let them know that they can rely on your support, not that you can just make them laugh.
- Be sure to apologize for your actions when you catch yourself acting recklessly, greedily, or insensitively.
- Make sacrifices — your wife's work dinner may seem way less fun than Star Wars trivia night, but let your partner know that you care for them more than you care for your enjoyment.

__Thriving at Work__ — Sevens are masters when it comes to finishing short-term projects or finding the root of problems, but they also need to keep in mind that they will need to bring more consistent results to the table if they truly wish to thrive at work:

1. When you catch yourself fantasizing about a promotion or a better future, slowly bring your focus back to your work. Remember, you cannot get there without some effort.
2. Don't pass on new opportunities because you fear the result. Your fear may not come naturally to you, but it is there — pushed deep inside. Before you say *No* or turn away from something, ask yourself why you are doing that. Do you really have better plans? Distracting yourself so you don't end up hurt is not an answer!
3. Make a list of all the reasons why your job is important to you — read them aloud when you start to feel suffocated and crave change.

Jobs and Career Paths: Many Sevens are entrepreneurs because ideas and creativity come naturally to them. Many are also failed entrepreneurs because making long-term ties and committing are not their strongest suits. To succeed, you have to learn how to focus and get a good team around you to execute.

The dream job of a Seven provides creative freedom. Think actor, life coach, blogger, bartender or bar owner, DJ, travel writer, small business owner, etc. The worst job for a Seven would be anything that requires hardcore consistency and tons of paperwork, such as accountant, lawyer, working in the customer service industry, etc.

Activities and Hobbies: Type 7s usually have many hobbies and pastimes. You like to fill your life with fun and experiences. You enjoy parties or dinner parties, reading (you get to explore new worlds), storytelling or standup comedy, cooking (especially rich, even gourmet food), music shows. Many Sevens love Instagramming or going on Pinterest, as they are full of inspirational, aspirational images and ideas.

SPIRITUALITY

Spiritual Struggles: One major stumbling block in your spiritual path is your aversion to pain. Facing pain, experiencing it, and learning from it is key to anyone's spiritual journey. In a spiritual sense, pain holds "messages" about ourselves and the world, and leaning into that pain and processing it can help us decode these messages and make us wise, resilient, and strong.

Painful life experiences and difficult situations also grow these important skills and traits. It's important to make commitments and stick with them, rather than running away as soon as things get difficult. You are always looking to be satisfied and happy. The key to getting there lies in sticking with things and finding a renewed and reenergized passion and enthusiasm for them.

Because of your optimistic, happy-go-lucky view on life, it may be difficult for you to take a spiritual path seriously. But if you do, the rewards will be great, deep, and lasting.

Your Life Lesson and the Path of Integration: Your life lesson is that life can be abundant in the microcosm. What do I mean by that? Well, your tendency to scatter your energy across numerous different things is a search for *abundance*. This is a spiritual concept, a sense of "my cup runneth over," experiencing joy and prosperity and a free spirit. The problem is, you're just one person. You don't have enough time to experience everything to its fullest. You can only skim the surface of each thing.

While this can be fun for a time, it doesn't satisfy your deep need for abundance. What will, though, is getting to that sense through *fewer* things. To experience the right things deeply brings a sense of fulfillment and abundance that a shallow taste of everything just cannot give you. Instead of sipping from 10 different cups, drink deeply from one. You have a sense of missing out, which makes you flit from one thing to another. But you can redirect that by accepting that *it's not a variety you truly crave, it's depth*.

Taking the view of depth as a good thing, you can create real progress in your outer life and in your inner life. You can take your visions and manifest them on Earth, which brings a sense of joy and fulfillment that is so deeply satisfying. This is where you find true freedom.

Daily Affirmations and Transformations for Type Sevens:

- I NOW LET GO of acting recklessly
- I NOW ACCEPT that I can perform best when I make centered decisions
- I NOW LET GO of exhausting myself so I can satisfy my compulsions
- I NOW ACCEPT that I should be moderate about how I act and what I consume
- I NOW LET GO of letting my insecurities lead the way
- I NOW ACCEPT that I can accept setbacks with a brave face
- I NOW LET GO of finding instant gratification
- I NOW ACCEPT that I should focus on finding deeper meaning in things
- I NOW LET GO of distracting myself with never-ending activity and adventures
- I NOW ACCEPT that I can be truly happy when I am calm and satisfied even with the small things

COMPATIBILITY — HOW WELL "SEVEN" SUITS THE OTHER TYPES

Type 1: As opposites, Ones and Sevens bring balance to each other. Since Seven is the growth line for Ones, imagine how well they may go together when a Type 1 is functioning at their best? Sevens help to lighten things up, which contrasts the heaviness that a Type 1 can fall into at times.

Type 2: Type Sevens are a positive influence on Two because they remind them to do good things for themselves, and to enjoy themselves. Since both types are sociable and enjoy connection, together they can be very welcoming to their community. Sevens may be pushed away by a Type 2 if they become clingy, as Sevens have a free-spirited nature.

Type 3: Both are energetic, optimistic, and friendly, so this is a good foundation. However, the Type 7s definition of success is quite different from the Type 3s. They have a much more relaxed approach to what it means to be successful, so they may be dissatisfied with the idea of missing out on the fun because of the Three's focus on work.

Type 4: Both these types have a sense of adventure, and Sevens can help Fours to have more new experiences. Fours often explore this adventure in their imagination, while for Sevens, it's all about real experiences. They both

3.7 TYPE 7 | 225

seek newness, in different ways, and Sevens can bring fun, positivity, and resilience, helping Fours through difficult times.

Type 5: Both these types love playing with ideas and debating, and can share a great sense of humor. A Seven can help a Five become more in-tune with the world through fun and pleasurable experiences, while a Five can help a Seven take themselves and life more seriously. The conflict usually comes from social styles — the Five thinks the Seven is too flowery, enthusiastic, and superficial. The Seven thinks the Five is far too serious and wants them to have more fun.

Type 6: This is a great pair, full of witty banter, jokes, and fun. Type 7s come up with great ideas, while Sixes have the organizational skills to follow them through. Sevens lift the spirits of a Type 6 and open them to experiences and opportunities. But when they're unhealthy, Sevens seem irresponsible and a weak foundation for security-seeking Sixes, while Sevens feel that the Six holds them back and is too negative.

Type 7: Two Sevens together can ooze happiness, fun, and radiance. They're a great company, within the relationship and with other people. They give each other a lot of independence. However, they may hurt each other with impulsive hurtful words, and have extreme difficulties settling down.

Type 8: Sevens and Eights have common ground in their desire to snub authority and revel in the physical world. They enjoy entertaining together, particularly showing their status and success to others. They both have high drive and can accomplish a lot together. If they don't have good outlets for their energy, however, the relationship can become very dark and even physically abusive.

Type 9: Sevens and Nines both have a positive outlook on life, are sociable and friendly, and avoid conflict. Seven brings the fun and glamor, and Nine enjoys being the audience. The problem is, they both blame each other for problems in their relationship and can't talk through their feelings. The Seven gets angry, the Nine withdraws.

MISIDENTIFICATION

Type 7s are often mistaken as Type 2s. This is because they're both very friendly and charming and because they both have an emotional intensity and enthusiasm about them. However, Sevens show a huge range of emotions intensely, including anger, whereas this would be rare for a Two unless they were under extreme stress. Another difference is that Twos want to be highly emotionally involved in other people's lives, whereas Type 7 generally just wants the company. They can be devoted, but they are never clingy like a Two.

A Type 7 might think they are a Three because both types are assertive and both seek success and luxury. The key difference is that Type 7s want success and luxury to feel alive, while Threes want them as a status symbol.

AN OUTSIDER'S GUIDE TO TYPE 7S

Let's chat! Stimulating conversation, jokes, debates... I love it all. The more, the better. I also want companionship and affection, but I really value my independence and my freedom. I don't like it when people are needy or clingy, as it makes me feel trapped. Give me my space, and I'm sure we'll enjoy many happy times together.

I'll really like it if you listen to my stories and my grand plans for the future. I love explaining my ideas and visions and chatting about them further. Ask me for more information, make me think more in-depth.

Whatever's on your mind, just don't tell me what to do! I'm pretty much guaranteed to do the opposite.

Type 8

The Big Boss

At their BEST:

strong
decisive
protective
independent
authoritative
direct
self-confident

At their WORST:

aggressive
insensitive
confrontational
intimidating
controlling
impatient
demanding

Shareable Quote:

I am the strongest and fiercest person you'll ever meet —
I come to win, not just to compete.
If you challenge me, it will only push me to the top;
when I smell power, I'm not sure I know how to stop.
I apologize if I intimidate or sometimes seem cold,
I just want us to feel secure, so control I always hold.

3.8 TYPE 8

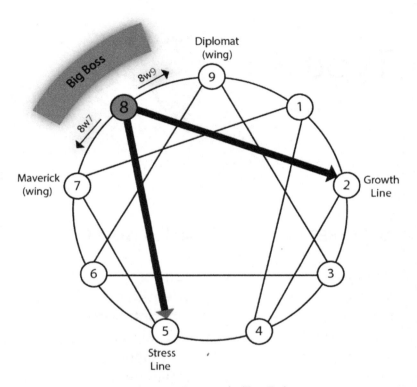

Enneagram Diagram for Type Eight

Name: Type 8 — The Big Boss

AKA: The Challenger, The Leader, The Protective Challenger, The Confronter, The Protector

Personality: Eight is the type of person that everyone secretly wishes to be like. They're ballsy, unafraid, and can win any argument. When an Eight walks into a meeting, the whole team lowers their heads a bit and start shooting puppy-dog eyes to win their affection. They own their presence when they step into a room because the confidence and energy that Eights radiate is almost hypnotizing.

If you're a Type 8, then you probably already knew it, even without taking an Enneagram test. Eight is the most energetic, hungry-for-life Enneatype, and they are born to be a leader. Not because they crave the power or authority, but because they need to be self-reliant and free, not to have someone telling them what to do, or breathing down their neck.

As an Eight, you're honest, independent, and decisive. You want others to see you as strong, generous, and fair, like a protective and powerful figure they can look up to. You exude confidence and charisma and inspire the same in others with your can-do attitude and direct manner. You know you can get through anything, and take pride in your mental, emotional, and physical strength. In fact, you relish challenges and will take them on as a show of force.

When life gives Eight lemons, they don't make a lemonade stand (that sounds a lot like Three, though). They plant lemon trees, so there are enough lemons for everyone. Yes, fortunately for all of us, Eights are actually considerate and justice-oriented.

If you're an Eight, you feel you must control your environment and remain steadfast at all times. Vulnerability is a sign of weakness. Underneath your exterior, though, you're playful, innocent, and gentle, which surprises many people. Many do not get to see that side of you at all.

At your best, you can be a true hero. You have a strong sense of honor and will go to great lengths to protect "your people." You will fight for justice for the underdog and the weak. At your worst, you can be domineering and aggressive, with a tendency for bullying. Yes, Eight can be the type of person who, after a month of living together, will have banned most of your possessions from the apartment, chosen all your furniture, and taken complete control over the remote.

Your Worst Fear: That someone else will take over the throne and start controlling you. Holding all of the strings is the only way Eight can truly be happy. Losing the crown scares them the most because they do not want to be perceived as weak or vulnerable.

Your Heart's Desire: To protect yourself and feel in total control of your destiny. Eight wants to be the boss, whether on a professional or personal level because that is the only way they feel secure.

Your Biggest Sin: Being hostile. Eight can act as though they are larger than life. The influence they exert does not only intimidate others but also makes them seem cold-hearted at times. Their directness can sometimes make them blunt and insensitive toward others.

Wings:

8w7 The Maverick — You're extremely motivated, and use your aggression and inner power to meet all your goals. You can accumulate great wealth or resources, and also spend a lot of money to have the best life has to offer, but without getting into debt you can't pay off. An Eight with a Seven wing is the real wild card on the Enneagram, with a true zest for life. You live your life to the fullest — ambitiously, but not afraid of taking reckless risks, either. The Seven wing here makes Eight warmer and friendlier, while still having a strong entrepreneurial side. You can be the boss everyone wants to hang out with after work.

8w9 The Diplomat — You're quietly in control of your environment. You have things done your way, but you dislike bullying or aggression. You sum up the phrase "an iron fist in a velvet glove," meaning you come across as gentle and peace-making, and you are, but underneath this, there is a strong will — you *will* get your way. You have an aura of quiet strength, and don't need to assert your power in every situation. You adore children, animals, nature, and the arts. The Nine wing gives you a balanced and more measured approach to life, and it also softens up the competitive side so you're as open to cooperation as you are to winning.

Subtypes:

Self-preservation Type 8 — The Survivalist

You are generous with your family or immediate circle, but much less so with others. You're focused on ensuring that you control as much as you can of your environment to make sure you and those close to you are safe and provided for. Your main lust for life is expressed through gathering material needs for your survival, and you can go against whatever you have to in order to achieve that.

The self-preservation Eight is a no-nonsense kind of person with an extremely uncanny ability to bargain and get the upper hand. You are mindful of your spending, but you are neither a cheapskate nor a hoarder. You just feel a strong need to get what you think you deserve so that you feel secure and financially protected.

Social Type 8 — The Group Leader (the countertype)

You are steadfast in your morals and champion a cause or causes. Friends mean a great deal to you, and you put forward your energy to win them. You have an aura of enthusiasm and power that attracts people to you. The only problem is that you're very other-focused, which can make you blind to your personal needs.

This countertype is called *the social antisocial* and with a good reason. The group leader is focused on protection and loyalty but also feels the need to go against the social norms. Social Eights are less aggressive than the survivalist and much friendlier, so they are often mistaken for another Enneatype. Male social Eights are usually mistaken for a Nine, while female social Eights are often misidentified as Two. However, the powerful traits of Eight, such as expressing power, engaging in conflict, and supporting others, are still quite dominant.

Sexual Type 8 — The Commander

You take possession of people and things. People tend to do what you say and submit to your will. You dominate your environment almost completely. But secretly, you desire a partner with whom you can be vulnerable and surrender.

You are a provocative rebel, not very social, and surprisingly, the most emotional of all Eights. You steal the show in the most charismatic way possible and often use your seductiveness to get and maintain control. The sexual Eight is unlikely to be confused with another Enneagram type.

Stress Number: 5. When you're under stress and not feeling good, you withdraw and become suspicious and fearful of people, just like an unhealthy Five. You become secretive, hiding your light and your energy, and feel paranoid about people hurting and controlling you. You may even start neglecting your own needs and welcome insomnia into your life.

Growth Number: 2. When you're in a good place, you become very open-hearted and caring, taking on the best qualities of Type 2. You're a shoulder for someone to cry on, and you give genuine empathy and understanding. A secure Eight doesn't claim that only their beliefs are right, but are open to and value the opinions of other people, as well. When they're in a good place, they even let others take care of them for a while, which is a huge step forward.

Center: You're in the Gut, Instinctual, or Anger Center. You express yourself in a direct and open manner, but your main emotion is anger, which you externalize. You are out of touch with your center and you are mainly angry at others, not yourself. Even though you're not aware of it, the people in your life are on the receiving end of it.

Famous 8s: Winston Churchill, Franklin D. Roosevelt, Pablo Picasso, Martin Luther King Jr., Fidel Castro, Julius Caesar, Courtney Love, Saddam Hussein, Serena Williams, Queen Latifah, Pink, Dr. Phil, Darth Vader (*Star Wars*), Don Corleone (*The Godfather*), Donald Trump, Napoleon Bonaparte, Nicolae Ceausescu.

Shareable Quote: *I am the strongest and fiercest person you'll ever meet — I come to win, not just to compete. If you challenge me, it will only push me to the top; when I smell power, I'm not sure I know how to stop. I apologize if I intimidate or sometimes seem cold, I just want us to feel secure, so control I always hold.*

MY INNER WORLD

What I Like About Being this Type: I like being self-reliant and independent. I know I can take on challenges, and I'm brave, honest, and just. I want to see those close to me do well, and I enjoy supporting, protecting, empowering, and encouraging them.

What's Hard About Being this Type: Sometimes, I scare people away when I don't mean to, as they find my personality too blunt or brash. I dislike it very much when people don't appreciate me when I've gone out of my way to help. I don't like that so many other people are so weak — I wish they'd just stand up for themselves!

Your Personal Vices (addictions): You like to be in control, so it's unlikely you'll use much in the way of drugs. Rich foods, alcohol, and cigarettes are more likely to be your downfall. When not healthy, neglecting your needs and missing medical checkups can also be your weakness.

Typical Thinking Patterns: You're constantly looking to exert your influence and strong will. You know what needs to be done — now you need the people to do it. You don't want anyone to control you, so you are constantly looking for signs of people doing so, and then batting them back down.

Typical Feeling Patterns: You would never let your emotions get the better of you unless it's rage. You tend to feel frustration and anger when faced with injustice, or people trying to control you or not respecting you. However, you yearn for someone to be vulnerable with.

SELF-DEVELOPMENT

When You're Very Healthy (levels 1 to 3): You're generous, courageous, and self-confident. You submit yourself to a higher authority (God, The Universe, a vision, or cause), and through this, master yourself. You have a passionate inner drive and are a natural leader. You may even go down in the history books for your great acts of heroism! You can be someone people can look up to — think Angela Merkel.

When You're Very Unhealthy (levels 7 to 9): You feel invincible, but you're also dictatorial bullying, and even possibly a criminal. You become hard-hearted and immoral — only your will rules. You can become extremely vengeful, sociopathic, and even murderous. If you continue walking down this path, you can become someone people will want to steer clear of — think Stalin.

When You're Somewhere in Between (levels 4 to 6): You're focused on not being accountable to others, making sure you're self-sufficient financially and emotionally. You work exceptionally hard but ignore your own emotions. You dominate your environment as the "boss," being boastful and aggressive and imposing your will on everyone and everything. Others are secondary to you, not equals.

How to Maximize Your Potential: You have immense personal power and will. But your true potential comes when you can uplift and inspire people, not dominate them and force them to do what you want. Underneath your bravado, you are truly innocent and pure, and showing this to people will help you win hearts, not grudging obedience.

Red Flags to Watch Out For: Believing the world is against you can lead you to really bad behaviors. Being very focused on power in every single interaction. Stuffing your feelings down and refusing to be vulnerable. Not wanting to take any advice or direction from anyone — your ego is large, and this can be dangerous for you.

Self-Development Activities: The biggest problem that Eight has is with their ego, power-oriented, and always-guarded personality. They are afraid to be perceived as vulnerable and anything less than strong, so they always press their real feelings down and walk around with a brave mask all day long. While this is what usually gets the job done, it can also get the *real Eight* lost along the way. Practicing self-development is what nurtures the true feelings and balances it all for a really content life.

Balancing Your Beliefs — Okay, okay, I know you must be thinking, "Come on, I am always right," but what if you are not? Or even better, what if you are not wrong, but someone else has an even better idea? Should you miss out on the chance of doing something better just because you didn't come up with the solution yourself? One of the best things you can do is learn how to balance your will and vision with that of others. Other people have great ideas, too, and if you can merge and blend your thoughts with theirs, you can become really unstoppable. And guess what? They will even respect you more.

To do this, slow down and take the time to listen to other people, not seeing their ideas or will as things in your way you have to get rid of, but as potentially valuable contributions. And no, you will not sound _weak_, you will actually be _more appreciated_. Use your powers of discernment to work out how best to go forward, then make your decision.

Nurture Your Inner Child — Inner what!? I know you must hate the idea of acting as a child, but I am not really talking about making snow angels here. I am talking about not overthinking everything and allowing yourself to detach from your obligations for a few moments, just so you can tend to your inner satisfaction. Like a child would ditch their homework for a chance of playing in the snow, you don't always have to be so preoccupied with doing. You shouldn't be irresponsible either, but pausing to do something you truly enjoy wouldn't really kill you. Drive to the coast and spend half of an hour doing nothing but watching the waves. Go to the park, take your shoes off, and feel the grass tickling your feet. Watch a really shallow movie, just for fun. Have fun!

Stop Black-and-White Thinking — Life is not all about *either you win or you go home a loser*. Not everything is either/or, black or white. There are lots of shades in between these two extremes; you just have to take off your power-tinted glasses to see. You may fall, but you will also learn a lot from the experience, meet new people, share some thoughts, grow as a person. Then you'll work to improve and get better for next time. See? Pretty colorful!

Double-Check Your Anger — When you get all fired up, stop a second before acting and ask yourself why you are really feeling that way. Does your aggression come as a distraction? Do you do it so you can hide your vulnerabilities? What are you feeling vulnerable about? Why are you hurt? Recognize these emotions and allow yourself to really feel them to find a healthy way to work past this.

Doing Your Best in Relationships — Your power-oriented actions and pure hostility can sabotage the relationships in your life. Although you mainly do this unintentionally, without actually knowing or wanting to do so, but you truly intimidate people and give off the impression that you care about nothing else but being in control. This can really hurt the people you love. To avoid being perceived as insensitive, work on your relationship with others:

- Stop alienating people. Try opening your heart to those who love you. Let them give you their affection and care. Pause for a moment to consider who is truly on your side, then make an effort to interact with them on a deeper level. Create a space that is not will-driven, and relax with them.
- Learn that vulnerability can also be a part of strength. Showing your tender side (which can be gigantic, by the way) to other people and being vulnerable with them will strengthen your relationships with them. See? Vulnerability equals strength, sometimes.
- When your lust starts taking over, have a friend be your voice of reason and let you know. Then knock down your power-grabbing tendencies a bit, balancing out your feelings.
- Don't get all defensive and impulsive with the people you care about. Remember, your words can really sting, so choose them carefully.

Thriving at Work — Although they can usually be found in the top spot, just like with the other Enneatypes, Eight also has some improving to do to really thrive at work. Here are the three golden rules that Eight should follow:

1. Heading toward the top is ambitious, but it's not positive if you do it by knocking others out of the road. Be mindful of how you're getting there.

2. Learn to apologize — Your control-oriented personality is mostly focused on dealing with situations at work, but that doesn't give you the right to run others over. Realize when you're getting harsh and offer your sincere apologies to those you've hurt.

3. You don't always have to be the rebel, just like the authority figure is not always the villain.

Jobs and Career Paths: Common career paths for Type 8s include activism, military service, executives, business owners, director of sales, athletes, politics, head of publicity, and, well, head of anything, really. The dream job here would be anything that puts you in a powerful position.

The worst job for an Eight would be pretty much anything that offers no (or very little) room for growth. Eight would feel suffocated if they had to work in a boring and closely monitored position, such as those of most entry-level administrative professions.

Activities and Hobbies: You may have very physical hobbies, like rock climbing, surfing, weight lifting, and the like, due to your physical toughness. Eight is also a great candidate to train for a marathon or any other competition, really. Extreme sports may appeal. You also like debating and public speaking.

SPIRITUALITY

Spiritual Struggles: The spiritual struggles of Eight lie in two areas — will and vulnerability.

In terms of <u>will</u>, Eights tend to believe that their judgment is infallible. You *know* what needs to be done and will do what it takes to get it done. The problem is, *no one's* judgment is infallible. Because you carry out your will based on what you think is best with such power and force, it means that your mistakes in judgment can have worse consequences than for other types. The issue here is the lack of discernment. You throw yourself headlong into acting out your will, without the checks and balances in place to see if this is the right course of action. A connection to God or the Universe, and a growing skill of discernment, will help with this.

The other area Eights struggle with is <u>vulnerability</u>. You believe that if you show any kind of exposure and openness, you will end up being controlled and mistreated. But you cannot possibly know that. Sometimes this might be the outcome, but be realistic — most of the time, it most definitely won't be. This is also connected with trust. You do not trust other people to be decent and straightforward; rather you expect them to hurt you. This interferes with your spiritual path because there is exceptional power in vulnerability at the right place and time.

Your Life Lesson and the Path of Integration: Your path of integration is embracing your own innocence. You, perhaps more than any other type, have access to innocence and purity. It lives within you, under the surface of your aggression. It's likely this is the reason *why* you are aggressive, to protect this innocence within.

The problem is, you may be so disconnected from this innocence you cannot even see it anymore. It may feel safer to bury it. But in this purity lies a great deal of spiritual power. Looking through the lens of innocence, we can discern what is truly right and wrong, rather than what society teaches us about morality. This gives you a deep personal connection to spiritual truth. This emotional connection should be the source of your will — your judgments are formed in innocence, and therefore, are spiritually correct. This means that you will apply your choice and life force to things that are spiritually in-tune, meaning they will benefit you, the people around you, and the world at large.

Tapping into your innocence is the key to your power and progress!

Daily Affirmations and Transformations for Type Eights:

- I NOW LET GO of my fear to be vulnerable
- I NOW ACCEPT that I have tender feelings that others will respect
- I NOW LET GO of running over others to get what I want
- I NOW ACCEPT that I should be more mindful of others' feelings
- I NOW LET GO of everything that makes me angry or resentful
- I NOW ACCEPT that I should focus more on love and kindness
- I NOW LET GO of holding the power at all times
- I NOW ACCEPT that there are other great leaders and bigger authorities
- I NOW LET GO of being focused on my goal
- I NOW ACCEPT that I am the happiest when I am working to help others

COMPATIBILITY — HOW WELL "EIGHT" SUITS THE OTHER TYPES

Type 1: These two can be a powerful combination in fighting injustice. However, Ones may find it difficult to accept the Eights approach to morality, unless the Eight is very healthy.

Type 2: Type 8s are very practical. This brings balance to the emotional world of the Type 2. While Eights are able to pay attention to the Two's emotional needs, they can be seen as cold, since they respect autonomy and have a different attitude toward dealing with people in general.

Type 3: An Eight can in fact encourage a Three to become more in touch with their emotions. This is because Type 8s are very strong and sturdy, allowing the Three to let their guard down. Both types are assertive, whereas Type 3s are more diplomatic about it. So, this can be a good combination in business as well as in relationships.

Type 4: Both these types are intense but in different ways. They are both passionate and impulsive; however, this can sometimes lead to recklessness. Neither type likes to feel controlled, so any misunderstanding about one trying to pull the strings of the other can lead to conflict.

Type 5: Type 5 is a thinker, Type 8 is an action-taker, so you have a lot to learn from each other. You both love your independence and can have stimulating debates. The Eight will protect the Five, and the Five will advise the Eight. But in conflict, a Five resents an Eight for being too aggressive, and Eight disrespects the Five for being weak. This war-like cycle oozes rejection and dissatisfaction, which will most likely be the reason why the relationship won't work out.

Type 6: Both types are suspicious of the world and other people. Type 8s take care of their own interests, while Sixes build a network. When they get through each other's walls, they have a deep bond of trust. Epic power struggles can be a problem, with either an aggressive counterphobic Six or a passive-aggressive Six.

Type 7: Sevens and Eights have common ground in their desire to snub authority, and they're reveling in the physical world. They enjoy entertaining together, particularly showing their status and success to others. They both have high energy and can accomplish a lot together. If they don't have good outlets for their high-strung personalities, however, the relationship can become very dark and even physically abusive.

Type 8: You trust each other implicitly, and this creates quiet confidence and mutual respect. Two Eights enjoy depending on each other and admire each other's strength. But on the flip side, there are constant power struggles, flaring tempers, and stand-offs, which wear both parties down and deplete their energy.

Type 9: Nines admire the Eight's "can-do" attitude, while Eights find Nines soothing, relaxing, and nurturing. But problems come when the Eight believes the Nine is willing to be molded, and the Nine strongly pushes them away with their stubbornness. Nines are passive-aggressive, Eights outright aggressive, and this relationship can descend into a battlefield of abuse.

MISIDENTIFICATION

Type 2s often mistype themselves as Eights, especially male Twos. They are both dominating and forceful and passionate and seek power and influence. The difference is that Eights will make it clear they are in a power struggle with another person, while Twos will veil it in their concern or care for other people. Eights show anger overtly, Twos try to hide it.

Another type that can be confused with Eight is Three. Both are competitive and ambitious, but there are key differences. Eights are not afraid of failure, and they're looking to dominate, no matter how other people perceive them. Threes are looking for success so they can be admired, and tend to conform more to other people's expectations, as it is important to them to win the approval of others.

AN OUTSIDER'S GUIDE TO TYPE 8S

Trust is extremely important to me. Please do not betray my trust or gossip about me behind my back, as this would hurt me very deeply. I will be loyal to you and go out of my way to make sure you're okay. Please don't take it for granted. If you could acknowledge my contributions, this really helps, but you don't need to go overboard as I'll find it insincere.

You make me feel most comfortable when you're direct and strong in what you're saying, and carry confidence in yourself. I speak directly and assertively, too. It's not a personal attack — I just like to get to the root of the issue. Don't take my anger too seriously, or let me walk all over you. Stand up for your point of view and what you believe in, and you'll earn my respect.

Type 9

The Zen Friend

At their BEST:

peaceful
nonjudgmental
patient
easygoing
considerate
pleasant
cooperative

At their WORST:

lazy
complacent
stubborn
passive-aggressive
indecisive
spaced-out
withdrawn

Shareable Quote:

I merge and hold my tongue because I hate to fight,
but that doesn't mean that I don't know what's right.
I'll agree with whatever just to get along,
but don't try to push me around,
because I'll show you that you're wrong.
I am loyal, kind, and run away from a riot;
I like to be at peace and spend my time in quiet.

3.9 TYPE 9

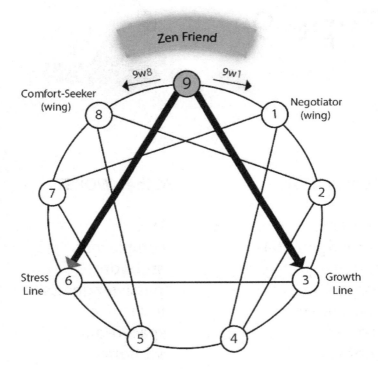

Enneagram Diagram for Type Nine

Name: Type 9 — The Zen Friend

AKA: The Peaceful Mediator, The Peacekeeper, The Peacemaker, The Comfort Seeker, The Healer

Personality: You know your friend, who somehow convinced you not to get out of the car and ask the guy behind you who has been honking at you for the last five minutes what his problem was? Well, that's your classic

Nine. A stickler for peace, kindness, and all things moderate.

Nine is calm, cooperative, friendly, and their zen-like personality helps them blend into pretty much every group of people. This is mainly because Nine hates quarrels and agrees to pretty much anything so they can be liked and accepted. But don't mistake Nine for a stooge! They may not upset the apple cart, but that doesn't mean they will allow you to push them around. Even though they are most comfortable with the *status quo*, they can get quite stubborn and start offering resistance.

If you're a Type 9, you're creative, accepting, stable, optimistic, and trusting. You are loyal and kind, and make one heck of a partner/parent. Give Nine the option of choosing between a fancy dinner out and a movie night on the couch with his family, and they would choose the latter before you even blink.

As a Nine, you are a joy to be around, but you can sometimes go along with others — or even "merge" with them — in an attempt to avoid conflict. You dislike any sort of competition, externally or internally, so tend to gloss over problems as if they don't matter.

Because you "go with the flow" so much, you might find it very hard to know who you really are or what you really want. But if someone takes advantage and tries to control you, you can get passively resistant.

At your best, you feel at one with yourself, know who you are, and are a powerful force of fun and joy. At your worst, you're totally ineffective, neglecting your responsibilities and becoming numb and unable to function. You can be a real *sloth* when it comes to tending to your needs. You are often in a self-forgetting cycle where you prioritize what others want and forget all about your own preferences. In an attempt to avoid rattling other's cages, you become neglectful of your feelings and emotions.

Your Worst Fear: That you'll lose people close to you and be separated from everyone.

Your Heart's Desire: To feel truly at peace. Being comfortable and in harmony is what Nine needs the most, so they tend to avoid conflicts and pressure situations to keep their calm state of mind.

Your Biggest Sin: Being passive-aggressive. You may not show it on the outside, but on the inside, you might feel like a loaded gun, getting ready to aim and start shooting. Nines often don't say what they think for the sake of keeping the peace, but that doesn't mean that things don't get to them. They are actually loaded with anger and resentment they haven't resolved. This can make Nine quite a dangerous creature — they can blow up when you least expect it.

Wings:

9w8 The Comfort-Seeker — When you think about it, this is probably the most confusing combo on the Enneagram. With Nine pulling to avoid conflict on one side, and the Eight rebelling against authority and trying to control on the other, it seems impossible that a 9w8 could be at peace. But, these contradictions actually seem to attract like magnets.

Nines with an Eight wing are sociable and easy-going with a large circle of friends. They are generous and accepting and have a genuine concern for others, but they also have tremendous inner strength and are very independent. They have a great sense of humor, are more direct about their needs, but are also spiced up with a pinch of aggression. When in an unhealthy place, their detachment can actually turn violent (emotionally or physically), without really caring about who they hurt.

9w1 The Negotiator — You have a desire to do the right thing and create harmony in your family, community, and society. You're orderly and well-mannered with a spiritual leaning, which brings you back to your inner balance through meditation, yoga, and practical steps toward personal growth. But you have a perfectionist streak that can lead to bitterness and you may also put up with abuse in the name of harmony.

The One wing adds a powerful sense about what's right and wrong, and this is the kind of energy that helps Nine stay on track, work on their confidence, and stop procrastinating. Although these Nines are more passive-aggressive than the rest, they can also be quite modest and just.

Subtypes:

Self-preservation Type 9 — The Collector

You focus on bringing harmony, order, and comfort through nesting and collecting. You like to read, eat, play games, sleep, watch TV, and build collections to comfort yourself, meeting your physical needs in a routine to find well-being. You use relaxing activities to avoid engaging with the world.

The collector also seems to need more time in solitude than the rest of the Nines. They are usually loving and kind, but deep down, they cannot quite feel like they are loved back. This is the strongest subtype of Nine, but this can also mean that self-preservation Nine is more stubborn and irritable than the rest.

Social Type 9 — The Benefactor (the countertype)

You participate with groups of friends and your community, but you can get lost in the going-along process. You sink yourself into different groups, losing your own sense of identity and direction. Your *sloth* here is expressed through merging with others' opinions and prioritizing the needs of other people over your own. You are loveable and easy-going, but deep down, you know that the root of your participation comes as a compensation for your deep feeling of *not quite belonging.*

The social Nine is the countertype because, despite their inherent laziness, they are very energetic. Dump them in an unfair situation, and they will have no problem expressing dissatisfaction and fighting for the good of the group, which makes the social Nine the best kind of leader.

Sexual Type 9 — The Fantasy Cadet

You see the world mystically, magically, and long for a perfect person to merge with. In this way, you're like a Four, only way less self-aware or self-loathing. The problem is, you don't want to lose your independence, so you create different relationships, usually two, known as "triangulation." You never fully invest yourself in either, and that is how you retain your freedom.

The fantasy cadet may sometimes even be confused with Type 2 because they lack that sense of self and use relationships to compensate for their self-perceived worthlessness. They have trouble connecting with a more meaningful aspect of themselves, which can sometimes make them feel anxious.

Stress Number: 6. When you're under stress and not feeling good, you become very anxious and worried, seeing the world and people as full of danger, just like an unhealthy Six. You start doubting your own actions and believe that the whole world is out to get you. On the plus side, when stressed, you become more reactive, which can sometimes be helpful.

Growth Number: 3. When you're in a good place, you take on the positive aspects of Three, becoming hard-working and energetic. You can become a role model and very successful. Healthy Nines take better care of themselves and are more in control of their lives. When feeling secure, Nine can be in true mental and physical harmony.

Center: You're in the Gut, Instinctual, or Anger Center. You have problems with anger, in terms of running away from it. You rarely participate in conflicts, and you'd rather just hoard aggressiveness inside. You avoid your center and its main emotion, anger, is mainly locked inside.

Famous 9s: Queen Elizabeth II, Abraham Lincoln, George W. Bush, Claude Monet, Carl Jung, Walt Disney, Janet Jackson, Whoopi Goldberg, Morgan Freeman, The Dalai Lama, Harry Potter, Dorothy Gale (*The Wizard of Oz),* David Beckham, Audrey Hepburn.

Shareable Quote: *I merge and hold my tongue because I hate to fight, but that doesn't mean that I don't know what's right. I'll* *agree with whatever just to get along, but don't try to push me around, because I'll show you that you're wrong. I am loyal, kind, and run away from a riot; I like to be at peace and spend my time in quiet.*

MY INNER WORLD

What I Like About Being this Type: I love the fact I can accept a huge range of people and feel comfortable with them. I also care for others and am concerned about their welfare, and I enjoy making these connections. I'm easy to be around, and people enjoy my company for the most part. I like the fact I can see many sides of an issue. I also like that I can let go and have fun.

What's Hard About Being this Type: I don't like that people don't take me seriously or judge me for being calm and easygoing. I sometimes hate myself for lacking discipline and a get-up-and-go spirit. Criticism also hurts me deeply, even in the tiniest doses. I don't like being confused about what I truly want, or feeling like people are talking over me or bossing me around.

Your Personal Vices (addictions): Overeating or under-eating can be a problem, also a lack of exercise. To escape anxiety and loneliness, you may reach for alcohol, weed, or other drugs.

Typical Thinking Patterns: You tend to always think positively and gloss over any problems or issues. You don't like thinking through or processing difficulties, so you tend to blank them out. You're also on the lookout for disharmony or disapproval, both of which make you nervous and uncomfortable.

Typical Feeling Patterns: You're typically on an even keel, but you can struggle very much with anger. This might be repressed anger, meaning you feel numb rather than actually angry, as it scares you to feel angry. You may feel sad or down without knowing why. You tend to bottle up your emotions.

SELF-DEVELOPMENT

When You're Very Healthy (levels 1 to 3): You have a calming and healing presence about you, and people want to spend time with you. You feel present and awake in the world, and this comes with a deep feeling of contentment. You feel very connected to both yourself and to other people. You're at ease with life and are optimistic and supportive.

When You're Very Unhealthy (levels 7 to 9): You bury your head in the sand about every problem and hide in the face of any emotion. You numb out completely and may not be able to function at all. You're dissociative and like a shell of a person.

When You're Somewhere in Between (levels 4 to 6): You go along with others to avoid conflict and agree to do things you don't want to do. You act how others want and expect you to act, and do not like showing your own agenda. In the face of problems, you tune out of reality and dip into fantasy.

How to Maximize Your Potential: Carefully consider what makes you different from others — what makes you *you*. This may be difficult if you've merged with another person or group. But one thing you can do is look for recurrent themes or interests throughout your life. Maybe it's music, or animals, or cars — anything that *you* take an interest in, regardless of what anyone else thinks. This will help you on the road back to you.

Red Flags to Watch Out for: Escaping into fantasy a lot — are you avoiding a problem that needs addressing or a difficult conversation you need to have? Other people treating you badly — you do not deserve any kind of bad treatment, and it is *right* for you to stand up for yourself. Feeling low for no reason usually happens because you are not allowing yourself to feel your emotions in different situations.

Self-Development Activities: Being a merging master and someone who likes to go along with things for the sake of avoiding conflict, the best self-development activities for a Nine would be those that would help them focus on what they need and want for a change.

Feel Your Emotions — Your emotions are *not* wrong. Sometimes you have an aversion to your feelings because you believe they create disharmony and conflict, which may be true. But the cost of holding your emotions in is greater — you become disconnected from yourself. This also means that the harmonious connections you have with others are, in a sense, not genuine, because they're not connecting with the *real* you. Think of your emotions as messengers, carrying messages about what is right and wrong for you. They can help you make decisions and get in touch with yourself more deeply. Don't run away from your feelings, but let them take over. Then try to encrypt the message and see what they are actually trying to tell you.

Keep Your Eyes on the Prize — Don't forget your goals and aspirations just because you've chosen to please others instead. Remind yourself frequently of the things that are important to you, so that you stay on track. Don't postpone them just so you can keep the peace.

Don't be Afraid to Ask for Help — If you cannot stay on task or focused enough to see things through, ask someone to help you to manage your chores better. This seems like something a One would be perfect at, so if you have a perfectionist in your life, let them give you a shot of their organizing powers and create a to-do system that will work for your needs.

Exercise — Okay, we all should be doing this regularly, but someone as lazy as Nine needs a stronger push in the right direction. Commit to physical exercise on a daily basis. This will not only get you out of bed when you feel like escaping, but it will also give you an energy boost to get other things done, as well.

Doing Your Best in Relationships — Nines are real sweethearts to be around, but their tendency to blindly agree to things can not only hurt themselves, but it will also stockpile anger inside that is doomed to burst out at some point. And whoever finds themselves at the receiving end of it can get quite hurt. To avoid all that, Nine needs to stop being so Nineish, and start doing things they are actually okay with:

- Learn to say what you think and stop numbing out. Your partner/friend will be less hurt if you would just turn the TV off (you know how "Game of Thrones" ends!) and tell them how you really feel.
- Say when you're not okay with something. You may think it will lead to a world-ending conflict, but it may seem like nothing but a minor disagreement to the other person.
- Be okay with saying NO. In fact, practice saying it. "Do you want to have a beer after work?" — "No, I'd rather go help my wife with the kids." It's easy. Try it out more often.

- Don't press anger inside. When something makes you mad, SAY IT OUT LOUD. Don't pretend you're okay with things you're not okay with. It's not healthy for anybody.

Thriving at Work — Just like with their relationships, Nine needs to stand up for themselves and share their feelings at work, too. These are the three golden rules for Nine:

1. Express your opinion. Even if that means going against what your boss expects from you.
2. Stay focused on *your* projects. Helping your coworkers is the Samaritan thing to do, but not if that means postponing your own work.
3. Remember that you are unique — people need to hear what you think. You can be an important part of the team if you bring your own ideas to the table.

Jobs and Career Paths: Careers where you can care for people, or spend time in nature or with animals, are often ideal. This might include working as a counselor, social worker, therapist, caregiver, youth group leader, teacher, non-profit director, human resources manager, religious worker, etc. The worst job for a Nine would be one that involves aggressiveness such as lawyer or investment banker.

Activities and Hobbies: You may enjoy meditation, yoga, music, animals, nature, napping, and chilling with your friends. Make sure you incorporate some exercise into your routine.

SPIRITUALITY

Spiritual Struggles: Your spiritual struggle is your unwillingness to face the dark parts of life, particularly yourself. You run away from what Jung calls the "Shadow." The Shadow refers to all the parts of ourselves that we have (or others have) deemed unacceptable, and we've hidden them away, not letting them be part of our normal personality. For a Nine, the shadow is large. You're such a kind, positive, optimistic, easygoing person, but the thing is, you're still a human like the rest of us, with a full range of emotions and intentions. This means that you'll have stuffed a lot of "you" into your shadow. Thus the kind, positive, optimistic, easygoing person is actually only *part* of you.

The reason we put things in our shadow instead of living with them consciously is that we fear if we show them we will be rejected or outcast. This is a real, continuous fear as a Nine. You don't want to upset others, because you might lose them, or at least lose the connection you have with them. It's understandable, but it comes at a cost — disconnection with yourself.

The parts of your shadow *are* you, and if you're to live a whole, real life, with true peace of mind, then you will need to reclaim them. Carl Jung, a famous psychologist and also a Nine, used the term "individuation" to describe this process. GoodTherapy explains, "Individuation refers to the process through which a person achieves a sense of individuality separate from the identities of others and begins to consciously exist as a human in the world." This is done through working with your shadow, i.e., bringing *unconscious* emotions, thoughts, and impulses to your *conscious* mind, becoming aware of them, and eventually owning them.

If you're totally unwilling to face pain, conflict, and unease, then you'll never get there. You will, in fact, be living a half-life.

Your Life Lesson and the Path of Integration: Your life lesson and path of integration is reclaiming your sense of self as an individual being. You're a master of integrating yourself, to the point of losing yourself, in others. This can help you tremendously in your spiritual path, as you become one with the Universe and God. But also remember, you're an individual human, a soul having a human experience. This means you have to have boundaries between yourself and others to be healthy.

Coach Sharon Martin explains, "A boundary is an imaginary line that separates me from you. They separate your physical space, your feelings, needs, and responsibilities from others. Your boundaries also tell other people how they can treat you — what's acceptable and what isn't."

To be able to create boundaries, you need to understand what your thoughts, feelings, needs, and responsibilities are. You have to claim them and separate them from other people's. You also need to get in touch with your anger, as this is a signal that people are not treating you right and that you need to draw a boundary. Anger is a very effective tool in helping you to draw boundaries and become your own person.

Daily Affirmations and Transformations for Type Nines:

- I NOW LET GO of always doing what others tell me
- I NOW ACCEPT that it is okay to be focused on my own needs
- I NOW LET GO of thinking that I cannot be accepted
- I NOW ACCEPT that I should express my thoughts and emotions better
- I NOW LET GO of always avoiding conflict
- I NOW ACCEPT that getting into disagreements is sometimes healthy
- I NOW LET GO of not being able to say NO
- I NOW ACCEPT that speaking my mind will not make others mad

- I NOW LET GO of pushing my dissatisfaction and anger inside
- I NOW ACCEPT that I should let others know how I feel

COMPATIBILITY — HOW WELL "NINE" SUITS THE OTHER TYPES

Type 1: Nines and Ones can go well together because Nines are more interested in harmony and don't feel the need to prove a point or engage in conflict. Nines are easier to get along with, so while they share many ideals with Type 1s, this allows for a smoother path. However, the passive-aggressiveness of Nine can sometimes blow up and bite One pretty hard. Ones don't do well with criticism and want to be in control, so this can catch them off guard and start a conflict.

Type 2: Type 9s are calm and easy-going. They are able to reassure Type 2s about their doubts, and offer acceptance. Both types seek support, and they are actually able to just *be there for each other*. However, the conflict here can arise because neither of the types can share feelings or make decisions with confidence. Also, when Nine's suppressed anger surfaces, it can cause Two to withdraw or lash out.

Type 3: Nines are able to help Threes to relax and enjoy more of the simple things in the present moment. They are also very supportive of Threes, and their easy-going demeanor brings balance to the Three's vigor. They teach the Three that they can be loved just as they are, and their worth is not based on their achievements. But if the goal-oriented nature of Three starts nagging Nine to be more initiative, Nine can turn to stubbornness and switch off.

Type 4: Both types are sensitive, but Nines bring a more calm and stable quality to the relationship. They respect each other's need for alone time but are emotionally available to each other. It's a comforting relationship for both but beware of the Nine's tendency to be a bit too withdrawn for the Four's liking at times.

Type 5: You give each other plenty of space, emotionally and physically. Nine respects the Five's intellect and curious mind, and it helps them "wake up" to reality. Nines can make Fives deeply relax and feel nurtured and safe. The danger is if both types are disconnected from themselves and start living in fantasy. The relationship does not get off the ground or have enough stimulation to continue because both parties are lost in their own minds and not truly living or being active in the world.

Type 6: Sixes and Nines can get along very well. They both want stability and peace of mind. They usually fall into line with normal societal values, and the counter-phobic Six can match the counter-cultural streak of the Nine. The two types, however, do not share their feelings, and this can lead to problems festering and not being addressed. This can lead to explosive rage on behalf of the

Six, and withdrawal or matched rage on behalf of the Nine.

Type 7: Sevens and Nines both have a positive outlook on life, are sociable and friendly, and avoid conflict. Seven brings the fun and glamor, and Nine enjoys being the audience. The problem is, they both blame each other for problems in their relationship and can't talk through their feelings. The Seven gets angry, the Nine withdraws.

Type 8: Nines admire the Eight's "can-do" attitude, while Eights find Nines soothing, relaxing, and nurturing. But problems come when the Eight believes the Nine is willing to be molded, and the Nine strongly pushes them away with their stubbornness. Nines are passive-aggressive, Eights are outright aggressive, and this relationship can descend into a battlefield of abuse.

Type 9: Nines often gravitate toward other Nines. You are patient, gentle, and supportive with each other, and this can be a lovely calm pairing, who also know how to have fun. The problem is that neither of you like conflict, so rarely have important conversations that could drive the relationship forward. Eventually, you can settle into a boring routine devoid of joy or excitement.

MISIDENTIFICATION

Type 2s and Type 9s can be confused. They are both very friendly, positive, and supportive, and enjoy being around people. There is a key difference, though — unless a Two is very healthy, their acceptance and support of others has a *motive*, which is to be needed, important, and indispensable. They also demand affection or respect back. Under stress, they become more aggressive, while a Nine will withdraw.

Fours and Nines can be confused because they are often both artistic and creative, and both types can be disconnected from the real world, shy, confused, and withdrawn. But the main difference is their outlook on life. A Type 9 is optimistic, a Type 4 pessimistic. Also, Fours are more likely to brood when they are upset, whereas a Nine will just think of something else. A Four's inner world is darker and more tortured.

The most common mistype for a Nine is a Five. This is due to them both being somewhat withdrawn. However, they are very different. Fives are argumentative, polarizing, and strong-minded. Fives are suspicious of almost everyone they meet, unlike Nines, who are much more trusting.

AN OUTSIDER'S GUIDE TO TYPE 9S

Don't take my kindness for weakness, please! Don't think you can push me around. I love to listen, to support, to be there for you, but don't take advantage or think you can tell me what to do. Don't put pressure on me or set high expectations — it stresses me out. I might take a long time to make decisions, but don't make them for me. I will get there in the end.

If you have something to talk to me about, try to do it in a gentle, calm way. I hate confrontation, so use a light tone and let me know we're still okay and there's harmony in our world. Physical affection doesn't go amiss!

ENNEAGRAM CHEATSHEET

TYPE OVERVIEW

TYPE 1 – THE ETHICAL SUPERHERO

Main Personality Traits: Over-Controlling, Perfectionism, Inner Critic, Righteousness

Worst Fear: Mess and Imbalance

Heart's Desire: Order and Moral Value

Biggest Sin: Being a control freak

Wings: Nine -The Idealist, Two - The Advocate

Subtypes: SP – The Money Maker, SO – The Collective Fighter, SX – The Compelling Preacher

Stress Number: 4

Growth Number: 7

Center: Gut

Driving Force: Anger

Emotional Weakness: Resentment

Attention: Finding errors to correct

Cognitive Conflict: Avoiding criticism and pushing for high standards

Cognitive Mistake: I (and other people) can do better

Self-Image: I am moral, accurate, and just

Deepest Longing: To be good and virtuous

TYPE 2 – THE LOVING ASSISTANT

Main Personality Traits: Generosity, Emotional Sensitivity, Nurturing, Sacrificing

Worst Fear: To be unappreciated

Heart's Desire: To be loved

Biggest Sin: Being manipulative

Wings: One - The Servant, Three - The Host/Hostess

Subtypes: SP – The Teacher's Pet, SO – The Ambassador, SX – The Lover

Stress Number: 8

Growth Number: 4

Center: Heart

Driving Force: Shame

Emotional Weakness: Pride

Attention: Presenting themselves like they believe others want to see them

Cognitive Conflict: Sacrificing their own needs to become likable and loved

Cognitive Mistake: You cannot *get* unless you *give*

Self-Image: I am helpful, warm, and thoughtful

Deepest Longing: To be loved and valued for who they are

TYPE 3 – THE RAINMAKER

Main Personality Traits: Goal-Focused, Success-Oriented, Competitiveness, Self-Deception
Worst Fear: Exposing the *real Three*
Heart's Desire: To be successful and valued
Biggest Sin: Being a phony
Wings: Two – The Charmer, Four – The Professional
Subtypes: SP – The Company Man/Woman, SO – The Politician, SX – The Movie Star
Stress Number: 9
Growth Number: 6
Center: Heart
Driving Force: Shame
Emotional Weakness: Vanity
Attention: Achieving goals to look successful
Cognitive Conflict: Liking their image more than they like the real Three
Cognitive Mistake: My worthiness is measured through my achievements
Self-Image: I am successful, capable, and competent
Deepest Longing: For others to accept and like the person hidden beneath the mask of success

TYPE 4 – THE ROCK STAR

Main Personality Traits: Prone to Suffering, Sensible to Aesthetics, Creative, Inferior Self-Thinking

Worst Fear: To have no identity

Heart's Desire: To leave a unique and significant mark behind

Biggest Sin: Comparing themselves to others, craving for what they think they lack

Wings: Three – The Aristocrat, Five – The Bohemian

Subtypes: SP – The Masochistic Artist, SO – The Shameful Critic, SX – The Free Spirit

Stress Number: 2

Growth Number: 1

Center: Heart

Driving Force: Shame

Emotional Weakness: Envy

Attention: Concerned with their inner experience

Cognitive Conflict: Seeking pleasure through pain

Cognitive Mistake: I dream to have the love I am not worthy enough of ever getting

Self-Image: I am emotionally deep, with a good taste and sense for aesthetic

Deepest Longing: For others to think that they are special and unique

TYPE 5 – THE ALPHA GEEK

Main Personality Traits: Overthinking, Knowledge-Seeking, Emotional Detachment, Hypersensitivity

Worst Fear: That you will end up depending on others

Heart's Desire: To truly understand the world

Biggest Sin: Holding back on your sentiments – Five would rather share knowledge than affection

Wings: Four – The Philosopher, Six – The Problem Solver

Subtypes: SP – The Castle Defender, SO – The Professor, SX – The Secret Agent

Stress Number: 7

Growth Number: 8

Center: Head

Driving Force: Fear

Emotional Weakness: Avarice

Attention: Gathering knowledge and preserving energy and privacy

Cognitive Conflict: The fear of depletion is what actually depletes

Cognitive Mistake: Socializing is exhausting

Self-Image: I am curious, private, and intelligent

Deepest Longing: For others to understand my needs

TYPE 6 – THE ETERNAL WORRIER

Main Personality Traits: Loyal, Doubting, Contrarian Thinking, On Danger-Alert
Worst Fear: Losing stability
Heart's Desire: To feel secure and safe
Biggest Sin: Extreme preparing for the future
Wings: Five – The Defender, Seven – The Buddy
Subtypes: SP – The Family Loyalist, SO – The Social Guardian, SX – The Warrior
Stress Number: 3
Growth Number: 9
Center: Head
Driving Force: Fear
Emotional Weakness: Anxiety
Attention: Forming allies and relationships to increase the feeling of safety
Cognitive Conflict: Looking for dangers increases the chance of finding them
Cognitive Mistake: The world is out to get me
Self-Image: I am loyal, hard-working, and prepared
Deepest Longing: To be protected

TYPE 7 – THE FUN LOVER

Main Personality Traits: Optimism, Adventure-Seeking, Hedonism, Impulsiveness

Worst Fear: Missing out on new experiences
Heart's Desire: To be truly satisfied without any ties
Biggest Sin: Fear of commitment
Wings: Six – The Entertainer, Eight – The Realist
Subtypes: SP – The Gourmand, SO – The Social Visionary, SX – The Adventurer
Stress Number: 1
Growth Number: 5
Center: Head
Driving Force: Fear
Emotional Weakness: Gluttony
Attention: Seeking pleasure in everything
Cognitive Conflict: Burying themselves in pleasures to run away from pain
Cognitive Mistake: Acting like they're *fine* without actually being *fine*
Self-Image: I am positive, adventurous, and fun to be around
Deepest Longing: That others will take care of them

TYPE 8 – THE BIG BOSS

Main Personality Traits: Being in Control, Will to Confront, Fighting Authority, Justice-Oriented
Worst Fear: That someone else will control them
Heart's Desire: To be safe and in charge of their own destiny
Biggest Sin: Being hostile

Wings: Seven – The Maverick, Nine – The Diplomat

Subtypes: SP – The Survivalist, SO – The Group Leader, SX – The Commander

Stress Number: 5

Growth Number: 2

Center: Gut

Driving Force: Anger

Emotional Weakness: Lust

Attention: Looking for the power to control

Cognitive Conflict: Running away from getting vulnerable only increases vulnerability

Cognitive Mistake: Thinking that you need to stay strong and undefeated at all times

Self-Image: I am tough, direct, and just

Deepest Longing: Not to be betrayed

TYPE 9 – THE ZEN FRIEND

Main Personality Traits: Upholding Peace, Easygoing, Avoiding Conflict, Over-Adjustment

Worst Fear: To lose the people in their life

Heart's Desire: To be truly at peace

Biggest Sin: Being passively aggressive

Wings: Eight – The Comfort Seeker, One – The Negotiator

Subtypes: SP – The Collector, SO – The Benefactor, SX – The Fantasy Cadet

Stress Number: 6

Growth Number: 3

Center: Gut

Driving Force: Anger

Emotional Weakness: Laziness

Attention: Avoiding conflict to preserve the harmony

Cognitive Conflict: Being comfortable with everything creates discomfort inside

Cognitive Mistake: Go along to get along

Self-Image: I am friendly, agreeable, and calm

Deepest Longing: For others to find my presence meaningful

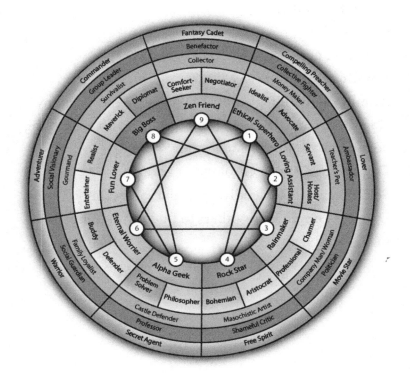

Enneagram All Type Names

SO, YOU'RE ENNEAWISE - NOW, WHAT?

First of all, thank you for sticking until the end with me! I know the ride was long, but I sincerely hope that the journey has been eye-opening and full of self-discovery.

If you've managed to tap into your long-suppressed and masked feelings, then you already have a pretty good guess as to where you stand on the Enneagram diagram. But, even though you think you've *found yourself* already, let me break it to you — you can be wrong.

Cracking the Enneagram is complicated, but what is even more complex is the human mind. We are not robots — we have the most hard-to-hack software. We change faster than the weather, and we grow every second of every day. So, needless to say, figuring out your Enneagram type is a bit of an art. To do it successfully, you have to consider many different factors, not simply answer a couple of questions and calculate the results.

For that reason, I've spent months researching and creating the most accurate test possible. It consists of six parts, it takes into account many different versions of you, and it can actually tell you your type, dominant instinctual subtype, and dominant wing (if you have one), all the while taking the growth and stress numbers into consideration. Plus, you get to double-test for increased accuracy, so you really cannot go wrong. Check out the second part of the book to see if your Enneagram-type suspicions have been right all along.

Lastly, even if you *do* find your type, I highly suggest you retake the test after a couple of years. Remember, we are humans, not machines. We change and are affected by life-altering situations. We make and break up relationships, we give birth, we adopt, we nurture, we become successful, we lose jobs... Every little thing that happens to us leaves a mark that can either push us further into the unhealthy traits of our type or make us healthier. While your type stays the same throughout your whole life, you can switch subtypes and wings. Remember, you will always share the main characteristic of your type, however, there are other little things that spice up your personality as well. To truly understand why something is happening to you at a given moment, you will need to have knowledge of where you are standing at that time.

Flying with balanced wings and leaning toward your left will set a slightly different course if you get my meaning.

The Enneagram makes all the sense in the world when you find yourself in it, but that doesn't mean that you should live your life obsessing over your personality traits. And it shouldn't bring resentment either. So, you've just realized that you've lost many years focused on all the wrong things, so what? Instead of beating yourself up over what cannot be controlled, try to use your Enneagram knowledge to set the healthy foundations for your Emotional Intelligence. Because, regardless of what type we are, we all want the same thing. And that is to identify our patterns of thinking and acting so we can actually control our direction.

And that's what the Enneagram does, really. It gives you the keys, puts you in the driver's seat, and lets you set the course for a change. It is up to you how long you will be the one driving. If you stay focused on your underlying motivation and try to shape your emotions and thoughts with why-do-I-do-the-things-I-do in mind, I assure you that you will have your hands on the wheel for life. All you have to do is keep your eyes on the motivation road and not stray from that path!

Happy self-growing, everybody!

NAKED WITH THE ENNEAGRAM

PART 2

A Detailed, Accurate, and Super-Practical 6-Part Enneagram Test

INTRODUCTION

Whether it was the first part of the book that intrigued you and inspired you to take this test, or your new-found Enneagram passion that brought you here, one thing is certain — you have landed at the right place.

If you are reading this, then it is safe to assume that you have already scratched the Enneagram surface a bit, at least enough to get you here. With that in mind, I also guess that you already have a pretty good idea of what your Enneagram type is. But, despite your *Enneaknowledge*, it takes more than just a few description lines to pause what you are doing and say to yourself, "That is totally me." It takes the right questions, real-life scenarios, and most importantly, it takes a well-calculated approach that will open up your inner eyes and allow you to see the person that has been hiding inside — to see the real you.

I may not have the power to help you switch types (although that'd be something), but I definitely have what it takes to help you discover your Enneagram identity. Because your Enneagram is more than just your main type. It is your wings, your subtypes, you when you're stressed, you when you're healthy... And all of that is covered in this easy, practical, and super-accurate six-step test.

All you need for this eye-opening ride are pen, paper, and basic calculating skills.

Ready? Jump to the first part of this test, and let your self-discovering journey begin!

TEST A

YOUR ENNEAGRAM MATCH

Starting with your personality's backbone, the first thing we need to figure out is which Enneagram type (1-9) suits you the most. By calculating the top three types that align with your character, we will use this test as the base for discovering your one and only Enneagram type.

In this test, we have 72 statements. You have to decide if you agree with the statements or not, and you can pick from 5 options depending on how much you believe they fit your personality.

Grab a pen of paper and write 1 to 72 down the side. Then note your score next to each number.

This will make interpreting your results afterward a lot easier!

Or, if that sounds like a lot of work (hey, no one's here to judge you, Nine!), you can just request an excel at https://freebies.nakedenneagram.com/excel. All you need to do is enter the answers there, and it will automatically work out your results. No hassle, no fuss!

Ready?

Let's get going.

1. I am an ethical person with strong ideas about right and wrong and how people should behave in the world.

> I totally agree 5
> I somewhat agree 4
> I'm not sure 3
> I somewhat disagree 2
> I totally disagree 1

2. I love taking care of people and being nurturing and kind.

> I totally agree 5
> I somewhat agree 4
> I'm not sure 3
> I somewhat disagree 2
> I totally disagree 1

3. I am really quite different from most other people, with both unique gifts and unique flaws. I'm a very unusual person.

I totally agree 5
I somewhat agree 4
I'm not sure 3
I somewhat disagree 2
I totally disagree 1

4. I don't like to take people's word for things on pretty much any topic. I need to study and understand things for myself.

I totally agree 5
I somewhat agree 4
I'm not sure 3
I somewhat disagree 2
I totally disagree 1

5. I am a meticulous person and I pay great attention to details.

I totally agree 5
I somewhat agree 4
I'm not sure 3
I somewhat disagree 2
I totally disagree 1

6. I like to have structure in pretty much everything I do. A chaotic life might sometimes appeal to me, but really deep down, structure and order make me feel safe.

I totally agree 5
I somewhat agree 4
I'm not sure 3
I somewhat disagree 2
I totally disagree 1

7. My goal is to be extremely successful in whatever I set out to do, ideally better than as many people as possible.

I totally agree 5
I somewhat agree 4
I'm not sure 3
I somewhat disagree 2
I totally disagree 1

8. Security and stability are extremely important things to me, and I don't often take risks.

I totally agree 5
I somewhat agree 4
I'm not sure 3
I somewhat disagree 2

I totally disagree 1

9. I love to be on-the-go and having tons of projects and activities to keep me busy.

I totally agree 5
I somewhat agree 4
I'm not sure 3
I somewhat disagree 2
I totally disagree 1

10. I like order in my life - a well thought routine, a well organized and clean home. Everything should have a designated place.

I totally agree 5
I somewhat agree 4
I'm not sure 3
I somewhat disagree 2
I totally disagree 1

11. Not many people truly understand me, as I have an extremely complex personality.

I totally agree 5
I somewhat agree 4
I'm not sure 3
I somewhat disagree 2

I totally disagree 1

12. I am something of a role model because of my hard work and accomplishments.

I totally agree 5
I somewhat agree 4
I'm not sure 3
I somewhat disagree 2
I totally disagree 1

13. I often second-guess my decisions and ask a lot of people for advice.

I totally agree 5
I somewhat agree 4
I'm not sure 3
I somewhat disagree 2
I totally disagree 1

14. I would rather watch an activity and learn how it works in-depth before I try my hand at it.

I totally agree 5
I somewhat agree 4
I'm not sure 3
I somewhat disagree 2
I totally disagree 1

15. I am enthusiastic and optimistic about pretty much everything. Some people might call that 'scattered'. I just get bored sticking to one thing.

I totally agree 5
I somewhat agree 4
I'm not sure 3
I somewhat disagree 2
I totally disagree 1

16. If I think someone's going to hurt me, I'll make sure to reject them first, and in a way, they won't soon forget.

I totally agree 5
I somewhat agree 4
I'm not sure 3
I somewhat disagree 2
I totally disagree 1

17. I understand most people's points of view and am not often sure what *my* point of view is.

I totally agree 5
I somewhat agree 4
I'm not sure 3
I somewhat disagree 2
I totally disagree 1

18. When I find my jam-packed schedule overwhelming, I do my best to avoid my responsibilities and escape to fantasy land to keep myself from mentally suffocating.

I totally agree 5
I somewhat agree 4
I'm not sure 3
I somewhat disagree 2
I totally disagree 1

19. The thing that makes me the happiest is when other people appreciate my love for them.

I totally agree 5
I somewhat agree 4
I'm not sure 3
I somewhat disagree 2
I totally disagree 1

20. People say that I have a snappish behavior, but I just get really fired-up when someone is unjust – I feel it's my duty to defend other people.

I totally agree 5
I somewhat agree 4
I'm not sure 3
I somewhat disagree 2

I totally disagree 1

21. Sometimes I feel a burden to be the best in the room. Otherwise, I don't feel important or valuable.

I totally agree 5
I somewhat agree 4
I'm not sure 3
I somewhat disagree 2
I totally disagree 1

22. I have a ton of crazy life experiences and plenty of stories of adventures to tell.

I totally agree 5
I somewhat agree 4
I'm not sure 3
I somewhat disagree 2
I totally disagree 1

23. I find it really difficult to stop hurting when someone does me wrong. It cuts me very deeply and I might never be able to forgive them, even if I want to.

I totally agree 5
I somewhat agree 4
I'm not sure 3
I somewhat disagree 2

300 | NAKED WITH THE ENNEAGRAM

I totally disagree 1

24. I often say yes to things when I'd rather say no.

I totally agree 5
I somewhat agree 4
I'm not sure 3
I somewhat disagree 2
I totally disagree 1

25. I am a perfectionist.

I totally agree 5
I somewhat agree 4
I'm not sure 3
I somewhat disagree 2
I totally disagree 1

26. Being helpful to others is my number one priority.

I totally agree 5
I somewhat agree 4
I'm not sure 3
I somewhat disagree 2
I totally disagree 1

27. One person isn't enough to face life's challenges. You have to be part of a group to survive and get through things without breaking.

I totally agree 5
I somewhat agree 4
I'm not sure 3
I somewhat disagree 2
I totally disagree 1

28. Other people's opinions about what I do are irrelevant. I don't waste time thinking about them.

I totally agree 5
I somewhat agree 4
I'm not sure 3
I somewhat disagree 2
I totally disagree 1

29. Praise and positive attention from others is what motivates me to further levels of success.

I totally agree 5
I somewhat agree 4
I'm not sure 3
I somewhat disagree 2
I totally disagree 1

30. I feel anxious a lot of the time.

> I totally agree 5
> I somewhat agree 4
> I'm not sure 3
> I somewhat disagree 2
> I totally disagree 1

31. You can only be a good person by sacrificing your time and needs to attend to others.

> I totally agree 5
> I somewhat agree 4
> I'm not sure 3
> I somewhat disagree 2
> I totally disagree 1

32. The purpose of my life is to leave something behind so that people can celebrate my creativity.

> I totally agree 5
> I somewhat agree 4
> I'm not sure 3
> I somewhat disagree 2
> I totally disagree 1

33. I often feel like a suffering victim, at the mercy of life.

I totally agree 5
I somewhat agree 4
I'm not sure 3
I somewhat disagree 2
I totally disagree 1

34. I would love to achieve so much that people would write biographies or make movies about me.

I totally agree 5
I somewhat agree 4
I'm not sure 3
I somewhat disagree 2
I totally disagree 1

35. A day without learning feels like a totally wasted day. Learning makes me feel invigorated, energized, and excited.

I totally agree 5
I somewhat agree 4
I'm not sure 3
I somewhat disagree 2
I totally disagree 1

36. I learn practical things really quickly and some people might call me a 'jack of all trades'.

I totally agree 5
I somewhat agree 4
I'm not sure 3
I somewhat disagree 2
I totally disagree 1

37. I'd rather stuff my emotions down or numb out, to make sure I have peace of mind.

I totally agree 5
I somewhat agree 4
I'm not sure 3
I somewhat disagree 2
I totally disagree 1

38. I feel at my best when I'm 'in charge' of something and can be directive and powerful.

I totally agree 5
I somewhat agree 4
I'm not sure 3
I somewhat disagree 2
I totally disagree 1

39. I get annoyed when people around me won't do the right thing, even if their actions have no direct effect on my life.

> I totally agree 5
> I somewhat agree 4
> I'm not sure 3
> I somewhat disagree 2
> I totally disagree 1

40. I am highly driven to achieve my goals whatever it takes, even if it means making huge sacrifices in other areas of my life.

> I totally agree 5
> I somewhat agree 4
> I'm not sure 3
> I somewhat disagree 2
> I totally disagree 1

41. I feel comfortable when I am sad and blue – that is my territory.

> I totally agree 5
> I somewhat agree 4
> I'm not sure 3
> I somewhat disagree 2
> I totally disagree 1

42. I love to be the person who can 'see' and 'understand' people who others have cast off and rejected.

I totally agree 5
I somewhat agree 4
I'm not sure 3
I somewhat disagree 2
I totally disagree 1

43. I would rather go on a two-week class and learn about things that I am passionate about rather than have a 2-week tropical vacation and relax.

I totally agree 5
I somewhat agree 4
I'm not sure 3
I somewhat disagree 2
I totally disagree 1

44. I love to be a listening ear and a shoulder to cry on.

I totally agree 5
I somewhat agree 4
I'm not sure 3
I somewhat disagree 2
I totally disagree 1

45. If a group I went to was going to close down, I'd offer to take over management to keep it open.

> I totally agree 5
> I somewhat agree 4
> I'm not sure 3
> I somewhat disagree 2
> I totally disagree 1

46. The world is a really exciting place full of so many possibilities. It's really hard to commit to any one thing when there are so many amazing options!

> I totally agree 5
> I somewhat agree 4
> I'm not sure 3
> I somewhat disagree 2
> I totally disagree 1

47. I often give up my own agenda to go along with someone else's. I'd rather do that than have an argument.

> I totally agree 5
> I somewhat agree 4
> I'm not sure 3
> I somewhat disagree 2
> I totally disagree 1

48. I have always had a *macho* personality. I find myself to be tough, both physically and mentally. I think I can endure whatever life throws my way.

> I totally agree 5
> I somewhat agree 4
> I'm not sure 3
> I somewhat disagree 2
> I totally disagree 1

49. I'm very proud of my independence. Relying on other people too much for everything would compromise my personal power and strength.

> I totally agree 5
> I somewhat agree 4
> I'm not sure 3
> I somewhat disagree 2
> I totally disagree 1

50. I really dislike conflict. If someone's annoying me I'd rather not confront them about it. I'd probably just withdraw from them.

> I totally agree 5
> I somewhat agree 4
> I'm not sure 3
> I somewhat disagree 2

I totally disagree 1

51. I am a living Encyclopedia. While others are checking their Instagram feed on their lunch break, I am reading scientific journals.

I totally agree 5
I somewhat agree 4
I'm not sure 3
I somewhat disagree 2
I totally disagree 1

52. I absolutely _hate_ having nothing to do and being stuck in the house. Being bored is the worst thing ever.

I totally agree 5
I somewhat agree 4
I'm not sure 3
I somewhat disagree 2
I totally disagree 1

53. I love to come up with bold new theories that no one has heard of before.

I totally agree 5
I somewhat agree 4
I'm not sure 3
I somewhat disagree 2

I totally disagree 1

54. I am my own worst critic. I tend to beat myself over the tiniest possible mistakes.

I totally agree 5
I somewhat agree 4
I'm not sure 3
I somewhat disagree 2
I totally disagree 1

55. People close to me often joke that I have OCD.

I totally agree 5
I somewhat agree 4
I'm not sure 3
I somewhat disagree 2
I totally disagree 1

56. I tend to get overly dramatic and make a mountain out of a molehill when I find myself criticized.

I totally agree 5
I somewhat agree 4
I'm not sure 3
I somewhat disagree 2
I totally disagree 1

57. Some may say I'm a _hoarder_. I always buy or bring an extra of everything, just in case I need it.

I totally agree 5
I somewhat agree 4
I'm not sure 3
I somewhat disagree 2
I totally disagree 1

58. I have excellent persuasive skills. I always find a way to convince people to do something.

I totally agree 5
I somewhat agree 4
I'm not sure 3
I somewhat disagree 2
I totally disagree 1

59. I have a hard time opening my soul to the people close to me. I fear they would just chew my heart and spit it out.

I totally agree 5
I somewhat agree 4
I'm not sure 3
I somewhat disagree 2
I totally disagree 1

60. If you say this is *black* when it is clear that it is *white*, I will see no point in convincing you otherwise.

I totally agree 5
I somewhat agree 4
I'm not sure 3
I somewhat disagree 2
I totally disagree 1

61. I am afraid of things taking an uncertain turn, so I always have a backup plan to have no unpleasant surprises.

I totally agree 5
I somewhat agree 4
I'm not sure 3
I somewhat disagree 2
I totally disagree 1

62. My partner always accuses me of micro-managing him/her, but I just wish he/she would just do things *the right way*.

I totally agree 5
I somewhat agree 4
I'm not sure 3
I somewhat disagree 2
I totally disagree 1

63. I am an excellent host and take great pleasure in having people over.

> I totally agree 5
> I somewhat agree 4
> I'm not sure 3
> I somewhat disagree 2
> I totally disagree 1

64. I will be happier if I listen to slow music and walk in the rain than go to a music festival at the beach.

> I totally agree 5
> I somewhat agree 4
> I'm not sure 3
> I somewhat disagree 2
> I totally disagree 1

65. I love to be able to cheer people up with my presence and charismatic spirit.

> I totally agree 5
> I somewhat agree 4
> I'm not sure 3
> I somewhat disagree 2
> I totally disagree 1

66. I am never alone. I could go to the end of the world, and I'd still be able to make friends almost instantly.

I totally agree 5
I somewhat agree 4
I'm not sure 3
I somewhat disagree 2
I totally disagree 1

67. I always seem to tune off when having conversations with others. It's just that the stuff in my mind is far more amusing.

I totally agree 5
I somewhat agree 4
I'm not sure 3
I somewhat disagree 2
I totally disagree 1

68. I usually get clingy to the ones I care about. I just don't want to feel left out.

I totally agree 5
I somewhat agree 4
I'm not sure 3
I somewhat disagree 2
I totally disagree 1

69. I would rather tell myself how I feel about the situation than actually say the words in your face. I feel extremely uncomfortable when arguing, so I just pack these emotions inside.

I totally agree 5
I somewhat agree 4
I'm not sure 3
I somewhat disagree 2
I totally disagree 1

70. I am quite the rebel and often think it's my destiny to fight the authority, whether it is my boss or the actual government.

I totally agree 5
I somewhat agree 4
I'm not sure 3
I somewhat disagree 2
I totally disagree 1

71. I am not a *mingler*; I would rather make a few circles and observe before actually entering the room crowded with people.

I totally agree 5
I somewhat agree 4
I'm not sure 3

I somewhat disagree 2

I totally disagree 1

72. I got so good at showing my best side, that I believe people will think I'm a phony if they find out what the real me is like.

I totally agree 5

I somewhat agree 4

I'm not sure 3

I somewhat disagree 2

I totally disagree 1

SCORING

Well done! You've come to the end of the test.

Now we're going to score the test and work out which of the types you're most likely to be. Each question correlates with different types. So I'm going to run through instructions for each type to help you get your score.

Step 1 – Start with Type 1 and look at the questions it includes i.e. Question 1, Question 5, etc.

Step 2 – Find your scores (from 1 to 5) for each of these questions.

Step 3 – Add up these eight numbers, for an overall score.

Step 4 – Now, we're going to turn that score into a percentage. To do that, take your number from step 3, divide it by 40 (the number of questions – 8 multiplied by the highest score – 5), then multiply it by 100.

For example, let's say my total for Type 1 was 14. To do step 4, I need to divide 14 by 40. That gives an answer of about 0.35. Then I multiply this by 100 to get 35%. This means that I am 35% matched to Type 1.

Step 5 – Continue through all of the types.

Step 6 – Note down your highest scores, as these are possibilities for your main type, your wing type, and your type under stress or growth. Don't worry if that doesn't make much sense right now. It'll become clear in the next few tests.

Type 1
Question 1
Question 5
Question 10
Question 25
Question 39
Question 54
Question 55
Question 62

Type 2
Question 2
Question 19
Question 26
Question 31

Question 42

Question 44

Question 63

Question 68

Type 3

Question 7

Question 12

Question 21

Question 29

Question 34

Question 40

Question 58

Question 72

Type 4

Question 3

Question 11

Question 23

Question 32

Question 33

Question 41

Question 56

Question 64

Type 5

Question 4

Question 14

Question 35
Question 43
Question 51
Question 53
Question 67
Question 71

Type 6
Question 6
Question 8
Question 13
Question 27
Question 30
Question 45
Question 57
Question 61

Type 7
Question 9
Question 15
Question 22
Question 36
Question 46
Question 52
Question 65
Question 66

Type 8

Question 16

Question 20

Question 28

Question 38

Question 48

Question 49

Question 59

Question 70

Type 9

Question 17

Question 18

Question 24

Question 37

Question 47

Question 50

Question 60

Question 69

Okay, so now you should have your *potential* type. Your result might not actually turn out to be your type! It might be your wing or your direction of growth or stress. Don't worry, I'll explain this to you as we go along. You have three more tests to do to confirm what your main type actually is.

TEST B

YOUR HEALTHY AND UNHEALTHY SIDE

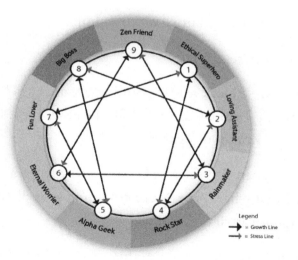

The Growth and Stress Lines

The Enneagram, as I've said before, is not a simple personality test. It goes deeper, able to explain your thoughts, feelings, and actions in *every* situation, even when you act out of character! Pretty amazing, right?

When you want to understand yourself more deeply using the Enneagram, it's important to know about Lines of Integration and Lines of Disintegration. There are lots of different terms people use to refer to these, and we're going to call them **the Growth Line** and **Stress Line**.

If you look at the diagram above, you can see a ton of arrows on each one. These show how we act when we're in a good place, and how we change when we're in a bad place.

It looks confusing, but I'll make it simple.

Let's say you're a Type 3.

You can see a black arrow pointing towards 6. This means that when Type 3s are mentally healthy, they show the *positive* attributes of Type 6.

Then you can also see a red arrow going from 3 to 9. This means that when Type 3s are not doing so well, they show the *negative* attributes of Type 9.

It's crucial to understand this, even when you're just working out your primary type.

Why?

Well, imagine you're a Type 3 but you're in a *really* good place in your life right now. You might end up mistyping yourself as a Type 6. And conversely, if you're in a bad place, you might accidentally have yourself down as a Type 9.

In this test, we're going to work out your lines of growth and stress. When you can match those two together, it'll be easier to make sure you've got your main type correct.

Ready?

Let's dive in.

You under stress

Pick one or two of the below statements that you think are true for you.

1. It's very important to me to do the right thing and be principled. When things are going wrong for me, I can get in very dark moods and nothing seems to make sense to me. I say and feel things that later, when I feel better, I don't think are true at all.

2. I love giving to others, being there for them, and caring for them. When I'm in a bad place, I can start demanding other people do things my way and being pushy about it.

3. I'm usually a massively driven person, but when I'm not feeling good, I feel disengaged and just can't be bothered to put any effort into anything.

4. I normally keep a fair distance between myself

and others emotionally. But if I'm feeling really bad I can get very clingy.

5. I love to learn about the world, but when I'm under stress I take on way too many projects and think about way too many things, my mind whirs hyperactively, and I can't get myself organized at all.

6. 6. I'm a person who is very loyal to my friends and beliefs. I would say the worst thing about me is that I can get very competitive at times like I or my group is the 'best'.

7. I'm usually playful and in good spirits, but when things aren't going well I end up nit-picking and not being satisfied with anything until it's perfect.

8. I'm usually a self-confident, strong person, but when I'm at my worst, other people seem really intimidating and I end up holding myself back a lot, being very secretive.

9. Peace of mind is hugely important to me and I try not to let problems get me down, but when I'm in a bad place I do a lot of worrying and feel really anxious.

You in a state of growth

1. On a bad day, I can feel angry at the way people do things wrong and don't stick to a moral code. But when I'm in a good place, the world feels much lighter and I feel like I can have fun and enjoy the great things life has to offer.

2. I usually end up running myself ragged looking after other people, but when I'm in a good place, I make time to think about what I'm feeling and what I need without feeling selfish for doing so.

3. Sometimes, I'll admit, I feel like stepping over other people to get to the top is necessary. But when I'm feeling really good, I realize that being committed to other people as well as my own success is really important in life.

4. I have a *lot* of deep emotions and life often doesn't feel stable. But when I'm in a good place, I don't feel so controlled by them, and I feel like I live from my principles instead.

5. I usually like to sit back and observe, but when I'm feeling good I feel more confident and able to participate.

6. I have a tendency to worry a lot and be fearful about the future, which leads me to tend to want to control things. But when I'm in a good place I feel much more relaxed and optimistic, and able to go with the flow.

7. I'm usually a ball of energy, wanting to take in as much fun and pleasure and experiences as I can. But when I'm feeling really content, I am able to slow down and focus. I feel fascinated by life and all its possibilities, but feel more able to pick a few things I really like, instead of abandoning things to try new stuff all the time.

8. In my heart, I just want to protect people. Sometimes people see this as controlling, but when I'm in a good place, my really kind and caring side comes out.

9. I'm not going to lie, sometimes I can be really lazy. It's just that nothing captures my interest enough to really commit to it and see it through. But when things are going really well for me, I feel much more excited about making my life better and taking the next step toward my goals.

You Under Stress – Answers

Now it's time to understand what your selections mean.

The numbers at the front of each of the statements actually correlate to that number type, so it's pretty easy to work out.

Find the number you selected below. So if you picked statement 3, for example, this is '3 going to 9'. This means that you're most likely to be a 3, as 3's show the negative traits of a 9 when under stress.

1 going to 4

It's very important to me to do the right thing and be principled. When things are going wrong for me, I can get in very dark moods and nothing seems to make sense to me. I say and feel things that later, when I feel better, I don't think are true at all.

2 going to 8

I love giving to others, being there for them, and caring for them. When I'm in a bad place, I can start demanding other people do things my way and being pushy about it.

3 going to 9

I'm usually a massively driven person, but when I'm not feeling good, I feel disengaged and just can't be bothered to put any effort into anything.

4 going to 2

I normally keep a fair distance between myself and others emotionally. But if I'm feeling really bad, I can get very clingy.

5 going to 7

I love to learn about the world, but when I'm under stress I take on way too many projects and think about way too many things, my mind whirs hyperactively, and I can't get myself organized at all.

6 going to 3

I'm a person who is very loyal to my friends and beliefs. I would say the worst thing about me is that I can get very competitive at times, like my group or I am the 'best'.

7 going to 1

I'm usually playful and in good spirits, but when things aren't going well I end up nit-picking and not being satisfied with anything until it's perfect.

8 going to 5

I'm usually a self-confident, strong person, but when I'm at my worst, other people seem really intimidating and I end up holding myself back a lot, being very secretive.

9 going to 6

Peace of mind is hugely important to me and I try not to let problems get me down, but when I'm in a bad place I do a lot of worrying and feel really anxious.

You In a State of Growth – Answers

Now look at the answer key below, and do the same you just did for 'you under stress'. So if you selected the '1 going to 7' answer, it means you're most likely to be a Type 1, as when Type 1s are in a place of growth they show the positive attributes of Type 7.

1 going to 7

On a bad day, I can feel angry at the way people do things wrong and don't stick to a moral code. But when I'm in a good place, the world feels much lighter and I feel like I can have fun and enjoy the great things life has to offer.

2 going to 4

I usually end up running myself ragged looking after other people, but when I'm in a good place, I make time to think about what I'm feeling and what I need without feeling selfish for doing so.

3 going to 6

Sometimes, I'll admit, I feel like stepping over other people to get to the top is necessary. But when I'm feeling really good, I realize that being committed to other people as well as my own success is really important in life.

4 going to 1

I have a *lot* of deep emotions and life often doesn't feel stable. But when I'm in a good place, I don't feel so controlled by them, and I feel like I live from my principles instead.

5 going to 8

I usually like to sit back and observe, but when I'm feeling good I feel more confident and able to participate.

6 going to 9

I have a tendency to worry a lot and be fearful about the future, which leads me to tend to want to control things. But when I'm in a good place I feel much more relaxed and optimistic, and able to go with the flow.

7 going to 5

I'm usually a ball of energy, wanting to take in as much fun and pleasure and experiences as I can. But when I'm feeling really content, I am able to slow down and focus. I feel fascinated by life and all its possibilities, but feel more able to pick a few things I really like, instead of abandoning things to try new stuff all the time.

8 going to 2

In my heart, I just want to protect people. Sometimes people see this as controlling, but when I'm in a good place, my really kind and caring side comes out.

9 going to 3

I'm not going to lie, sometimes I can be really lazy. It's just that nothing captures my interest enough to really commit to it and see it through. But when things are going really well for me, I feel much more excited about making my life better and taking the next step toward my goals.

Progress so far

Do your numbers from test B match some of your highest scoring types from Test A? If so, that's a little bit of confirmation for you. Have a look at your results and see what patterns you can find.

Let's say in Test A your results were:

Type 4 - 90%
Type 1 – 85%
Type 7 – 60%

And then the rest were all lower.

Let's say in test B your results were:

Growth:
1 going to 7
4 going to 1
Stress:
1 going to 4

What could this mean?

With these scores, you could either be a Type 1 or a Type 4. Remember, Type 1s go to Type 4 when they're under stress, and Type 4s go to Type 1 when they're in a state of growth, so it can be hard to tell between the two sometimes.

You might find that you're stuck between two types as well.

If the types are *next* to each other on the Enneagram, so let's say you're not sure if you're a Type 2 or a Type 3, then it's likely that one of these is your main type, and the other is your *dominant wing*. We'll be looking at wings in a short while.

If your types are *connected* by the lines on the Enneagram, it means, as you know, that the types are connected due to our personality changes in times of growth or stress.

Remember, you don't have to make a final decision about what type you are right now. If your results are clear and you can tell your type right away, then great! But if nothing is looking promising, don't worry, there are still more tests to come!

TEST C

GETTING DESCRIPTIVE WITH YOUR PERSONALITY

By now, you probably have a pretty good idea of your type. But if you're still not sure, then it could be useful to take this test. This test is a little unusual, as it doesn't have any answers for you to pick from. Instead, I'm going to give you writing prompts for you to write your own answers. Then, in the end, I'm going to tell you how you can interpret your answers.

Question 1: When you're feeling at your absolute worst, what kind of thoughts are going through your head? How do you feel? What do you believe about life and yourself?

_____

_____

_____

_____

_____

Question 2: *Imagine you're in your old age, on your deathbed, with your grandchildren and great-grandchildren, or other young family members, around you. They're just starting out on life. What life advice would you give them?*

_____

_____

_____

_____

_____

Question 3: *Imagine you're writing a book, and the main character is the best, idealized version of yourself. Describe their character or what they'd be doing in the book.*

_____

_____

_____

_____

_____

Analyzing

Ready to analyze yourself?!

In this section, I'm going to help you analyze your own writing to get a better understanding of what your type might be. We will also get a little insight into your wings and lines of growth and stress.

What I'm going to do is give you phrases, themes, and ideas that match each type. Then you can look for these in your writing. Each phrase, theme, or idea has *two* types written next to it. Why two?

There are two types because this (not so) cheerful question (!) is all about how we feel when we're at our *worst*. This ties in with our line of stress or disintegration. So say you're a Type 5. This means you go to the worst aspects of Type 7 when under stress. When you're feeling down, you are likely to have negative thoughts from *both* types, your main Type 5, and your 'under stress' Type 7.

Any time you get a theme or phrase that matches a type, tally the two types. By the end, you'll be able to see which type shines through the most in your writing.

Okay, let's jump in.

Question 1: *When you're feeling at your absolute worst, what kind of thoughts are going through your head? How do you feel? What do you believe about life and yourself?*

- I have evil inside me. (1, 7)
- I am corrupt. (1, 7)
- Being morally defective, other people, or the world being morally deficient. (1, 7)
- I am unworthy of love. (2, 4)
- I am unwanted. (2, 4)
- I could die tomorrow, and not enough people would notice. (3, 6)
- Everyone thinks I'm a failure. (3, 6)

- I don't matter at all, as a person. (1, 4)
- I am just a non-person. (1, 4)
- I need someone to save me by understanding me and loving me for who I *really* am. (1, 4)
- I am totally useless and incapable. (5, 8)
- I feel like I'm drowning and failing in trying to navigate the world. (5, 8)
- There's no one here to guide me and support me. (6, 9)
- I am so scared of doing this on my own. (6, 9)
- I'm missing out on so much. (5, 7)
- I just wish I could be happy and doing something enjoyable all the time. (5, 7)
- I feel trapped. (5, 7)
- This person is taking advantage of me. (2, 8)
- There is nothing I can do to take control of this situation. (2, 8)
- I'm so lonely. (3, 9)
- I feel empty inside, like a shell of a person. (3, 9)
- I feel so lost and directionless. (3, 9)

Count up how many times each number appeared. It's likely that the type that came up the most times is your *main* type. If you had two numbers that had an equal number of matches, then it's likely that one is your main type and one is your stress line. Check to see if that makes sense. For example, if you had a score of 5 for Type 4, and 5 for Type 2, it could well be that your main type is Type 4 because its stress line is Type 2.

If the types do *not* match up with the stress lines diagram, for example, if you had Type 5 and Type 4 both with high scores, then it could be that one of them is your main type, and one of them is your wing.

Now onto question 2. Again, it's time to analyze the themes found in your writing.

Question 2: Imagine you're in your old age, on your deathbed, with your grandchildren and great-grandchildren, or other young family members, around you. They're just starting out on life. What life advice would you give them?

- Do the right thing. (1)
- Be a morally upstanding person. (1)
- Work hard to make a change in the world and fight for a cause you believe in. (1)
- Family is the most important thing. (2)
- Be kind. (2, 9)
- Be good to each other. (2)
- Work hard to achieve your dreams. (3)
- You can do anything you put your mind to. (3)
- Express yourself and who you really are. (4)
- Be yourself and don't follow the crowd. (4)
- You are special and unique. (4)
- Never stop learning about the world. (5)
- Sharing knowledge or giving them books or

philosophies to learn from. (5)
- Make sure to make good friends. (6)
- Advice about security and stability. (6)
- The world is your oyster, so many opportunities and experiences to have. (7)
- Don't take life or yourself too seriously. Life is short, so enjoy it. (7)
- Protect what is yours and of those you love. (8)
- Control your own life and destiny. (8)
- Take on challenges and prove yourself. (8)
- Peace and harmony between people are the most important things. (9)
- Find your own inner peace. (9)
- Discover who you are and what is important to you. (9)

Note down which type occurs the most frequently in your writing. If you have two or more types that score highly, have a look again at how these types are connected.

Let's say you have high scores across types 2, 5, and 8. A quick look at the growth and stress lines diagram would let you know that a Type 8 goes to Type 2 in growth and Type 5 under stress. So that could indicate that your main type is Type 8.

Or maybe you have types 2, 8, and 9 scoring highly. That could be because you are a Type 8, going to Type 2 in growth, and have a Type 9 wing.

Okay, now let's move onto question 3.

Question 3: *Imagine you're writing a book, and the main character is the best, idealized version of yourself. Describe their character or what they'd be doing in the book.*

As before, identify relevant phrases and themes:

- Principled (1)
- High standards (1)
- Serious (1)
- Moral and honest (1)
- Hard-working (1)
- High standards (1)
- Improving things for others through causes and crusades (1)
- Nurturing and caring (2)
- Self-sacrificing for others (2)
- Warm and fuzzy (2)
- Highly-accomplished (3)
- Empowered (3)
- Entrepreneur, high-powered job (3)
- Looking good (3)
- Elite (3, 4)
- Beautiful and usual surroundings and personal appearance (4)
- Creative (4)
- Romantic or passionate (4)
- Dramatic (4)

- Eccentric (4, 5)
- Spiritual (4)
- Classy, sophisticated (4)
- Wise (5)
- Intellectual and complex (5)
- Expert (5)
- Cool and dispassionate (5)
- Part of a group (6)
- Loyalty, not usually in a leadership position (6)
- Themes of authority, going between rebellion and obedience (6)
- Security and stability (6)
- Adventures and multiple locations (7)
- Funny and entertaining (7)
- Charming, sensual (7)
- Rebellion (8)
- Aggressive leader (8)
- Protecting others (8)
- Street-wise (8)
- Fearless (6, 8)
- Outlaw (8)
- Harmony (9)
- Utopia (9)
- Many admirers (3, 4, 7, 8)

Again, calculate how many you got for each type. The one with the most *should* be your main type, but it *may* be where you go to in a state of growth.

TEST D

CONFIRM YOUR TYPE (FUN!)

You've got a *ton* of data now on what your type might be. Are you sure you've nailed down your main type? Or are you still unsure? Either way, here's a fun 'what would you do' quiz. Pick one or two of the below answers that you think are true for you.

1. It's vacation time. Do you...?

- Go to a place that is related to your special, unique interests? (4, 5)
- Plan an itinerary that accounts for pretty much every hour of your time? (1)
- Book the day before on a whim to a place you've *never* been before? (7)
- Make sure that *you* have the final decision on where your family will go? (8)

- Immerse yourself in the magic of the place and write poems about it? (4)
- Pick the most luxurious place you can find and plaster pictures all over Facebook? (3)
- Research how safe the destination is and local crime rates? (6)
- Give a trip as a gift to a loved one or friend and focus on what they want to do the whole time you're there? (2)
- Find a very unusual destination and delight in learning all about it and discussing it at length with friends when you get back? (5)
- Go wherever your family wants to go? (9)

2. Your boss has criticized your performance at work. What do you do?

- Go between feeling angry at them but not showing it, and very ashamed of yourself? (1)
- Feel incompetent and incapable, lose confidence, and hide in your room for the evening? (5)
- Go play a video game or read a book to forget about it? (9)
- Feel confused and anxious and wish you had a rule book so that you could do everything right? (6)
- Cry in the toilets? (4)

- Argue that your performance was absolutely fine and you were in the right? (8)
- Don't let it show you're offended, and take it on the chin? (7)
- Immediately make strategies for how you can do better in the future, and then show them to your boss and explain how you'll implement them immediately? (3)
- Feel devastated and immediately try to make amends and repair trust? (2)
- Ask for concrete examples so you can view the situation objectively? (5)

3. You're on a first date. What are you looking for to say yes to a second date?

- Someone who is stable and responsible (6)
- Someone who offers physical and emotional comfort (9)
- Someone who accepts my nurturing and brightens up when I compliment them (2)
- Someone who intellectually stimulates me (5)
- Someone who is idealistic (1)
- Someone who is adventurous (7)
- Someone who is very emotionally expressive (2)
- Someone who is well-dressed in conventional fashion (3)

344 | NAKED WITH THE ENNEAGRAM

- Someone who is well-dressed in an unusual way (4)
- Someone with principles and morals (1)
- Someone who is direct (8)
- Someone who makes me feel safe (6)
- Someone who has a beautiful, interesting way of perceiving the world (4)
- Someone who gives me genuine compliments (3, 4)
- Someone who is not pushy and respects the need for 'me 'time (5)
- Someone who is strong and confident (8)
- Someone with interesting stories (7)
- Someone who loves pets and nature (2, 9)
- Someone who treats me like an absolute prince/princess and makes me the center of attention (3)

Tally up all your answers.

Did your results match the type you thought you were?

As always, if you have more than one result, go back and check against the lines of growth and stress, or see if it could be your wing.

We're about to dive more into wings in the next test.

TEST E

A DOMINANT WING OR A BALANCED FLIGHT?

Your wings are your neighbor types spicing up your personality with some of their traits (both good and bad). If you are Type 1, your wings will be Nine and Two. If you are Type 2, your wings will be One and Three. You get my meaning.

If you cannot quite imagine this, just picture your wings as your actual neighbors. Imagine three houses in a row. You live in the house in the middle, and you have neighbors on your left and right. Now imagine your neighbors sitting on their front porches, shooting comments your way, and telling you what they think you should do or feel in certain situations. If you take the advice of one neighbor more than the other's, then that neighbor is your dominant wing. But if you use them interchangeably or just listen to their suggestions to shape your own decision, then your wings are balanced.

What I'm trying to say is this – you might not have a dominant wing. In fact, the point is to use your wings as support, but not to lean on either side heavily. *The goal is to have your wings balanced.*

Below, you will find a test I've created that will help you discover whether you have a dominant wing or you're balanced. But also, you can quickly get an idea of which wing is slightly overpowering if you are almost balanced.

Assuming you have already tested for your main Enneatype, take the wing test accordingly. There are four questions for each type so you don't even need a pen and paper (if you can remember four answers, that is).

TYPE 1

1. Your Friend is in trouble, and you can help them out. They agree to your assistance, but a couple of hours later, they turn down your help, explaining that they've found a different solution. You:

A) Understand that your friend has found a better way to cope with their problem.

B) Are a little bit disappointed that you don't get to save the day but feel happy that your friend will finally be out of the mess.

C) Feel frustrated that you are no longer involved – you believe that your solution is way better.

2. You have just got fired from your job. You:

A) Numb the pain and frustration with a bowl of ice cream and reality TV and might even throw a bottle of booze into the mix.

B) Feel that's unfair that you've got let go instead of others, but you believe you will find another job soon.

C) Know just what to do and immediately start making calls and arranging meetings.

3. Your boss has just given you tons of new work, even though they know you haven't finished the old projects yet. This has become a common occurrence at the office. You:

A) Throw your hands in the air and feel tired and exhausted from the unfairly distributed workload.

B) Think it's unfair, but don't say anything – you will think of a solution later.

C) Loudly object, making yourself a martyr to the extend of giving an ultimatum – either they will find a better solution of dealing with all the work-load, or you're out the door.

4. Your partner has forgotten your birthday (yet again), even though you've thrown them such a huge surprise for their big day. You:

A) Are tired of being unappreciated, so you detach and isolate yourself to get away from the disappointment.

B) Feel sad, but you let your partner know that you feel they should make more of an effort in your relationship.

C) Get frustrated and feel undervalued, so you make a loud scene, making sure your partner remembers just how unjustly you've been treated.

TYPE 2

1. You've just realized that you've made a huge mistake at work. You:

A) Take it out on yourself, criticizing your own actions, feeling angry for not being able to perform better.

B) Feeling disappointed that you have made a mistake but will try to do your best to immediately fix the issue.

C) Waste no time in feeling sorry for yourself, but ambitiously jump to find a solution as soon as possible.

2. You find yourself at an incredibly awkward party. You:

A) Try to see what is *wrong* with the party and what can be *corrected* so you can offer your help. Think there-are-no-more-snacks-I'll-go-refill-the-plate kind of help.

B) Try to mingle and see if you will find someone that will like to engage in a conversation with you.

C) Talk to the first person sitting/standing next to you. You will talk about the party, the weather, even politics or global warming if needed, just so you chat and be more social.

3. You and your friend have just parted ways and ended your relationship. You:

A) Immediately think it is your fault and start judging your actions. *If only I haven't said that to her/him.*

B) Feel really bad, but as soon as these negative emotions start piling up, you retrieve from this dark corner and include your mind into the action, doing your best to process what just happened the healthiest way possible.

C) Are extremely hurt and all over the place. Your feelings overwhelm you to the point that is hard to be functioning properly.

4. Imagine that you and your partner are having a huge fight with him/her criticizing your actions. You:

A) Think of your actions as always right and perfect, so you immediately start preaching about what you believe is right and wrong and try to rub your partner the wrong way.

B) Feel hurt that your partner feels that way, but you stop to question your actions and turn to your mind for help.

C) Feel like your pride has taken a painful shot, so you experience powerful anger bursts and arrogantly try to take over authority over the situation.

TYPE 3

1. You have a steady job and are a part of a good team. The thing that motivates you the most at work and powers your activities is:

A) The fact that your coworkers need you, look up to you and can depend on your help for support.

B) The fact that you are successful and can achieve so much despite being around other competent and hardworking people.

C) To have a sense of belonging and be accepted and validated by your team.

2. You've got so caught up with your workload that you completely forgot about a promise you've made to a friend. You:

A) Feel so bad because you fear your friend will see you as unworthy and undeserving of their love and affection.

B) Feel bad but do your best to find a solution that can compensate for the loss.

C) You feel bad because your friend will see you as a failure – as someone who cannot finish anything with success.

3. Your partner had just informed you that you will have his/her new colleagues over for dinner in a couple of days. You start asking questions about them so you can plan your dinner in a way that:

A) Will help your guests admire you and find you socially attractive – you hope they will think that the dinner may not have gone that good if it was someone else hosting it.

B) Helps you feel like a good host and makes them feel relaxed and satisfied that evening.

C) Makes you come off as *one of them* so they can accept you and value your hard work.

4. You are in for a big promotion, but you have to impress your new boss first. You:

A) Do your best to find ways to make you feel helpful and valuable to the team – you play on the the-future-of-the-company-depends-on-this-person card.

B) You put in a lot of effort, long work hours, and hope that you will be recognized for your hard-working and dedicated nature.

C) You do your best to *stand out* from your competitors and win your boss with your creative approach and out-of-the-box thinking.

TYPE 4

1. You've entered a competition of some kind, and you end up second. Your first thoughts are:

A) How could anyone be more creative than me?

B) I am sad I'm not the winner, but I will try to perfect my skill for the next time.

C) I knew I should have done something differently.

2. Your partner has been acting a little bit suspiciously. You:

A) Become obsessive – checking their phones and asking many questions with a tendency to dramatize their every single move.

B) You may get suspicious, but you need to hear it from your partner. So, you ask them what has been going on.

C) You are certain of the worst and withdraw within yourself.

3. Your friend believes that they should quit their job and start their own freelancing business. They ask you for advice. You:

A) Start laying out the risks of freelancing – unstable income, non-steady financial security.

B) Think that your friend has what it takes to thrive on their own, but ask them if they are ready enough to endure the challenges?

C) Rely mostly on the facts – your friend is a skilled and hardworking person, so they will surely succeed.

4. Your boss has just informed you that they will assign the shiny new project to your coworker. You:

A) Believe that that's a mistake because you are the only person who can execute it right.

B) Are a bit frustrated but will do your best to work hard and let your boss know you can handle challenges.

C) Start feeling like your boss hates you and let your negative emotions affect your work.

TYPE 5

1. You've been just let go of your job. You:

A) Are afraid that others will find you incompetent and that you may have to end up seeking help from family/friends.

B) Are sad but will use your knowledge and skills to search for better opportunities.

C) Find yourself feeling incapable and useless, letting your feelings of insecurity take over.

2. You've been working on a project for a long time, and finally, it turned out to be just perfect. That makes you feel:

A) Happy that others will look at you with admiration and appreciation.

B) Glad you could see the project through - you immediately start brainstorming new ways to use your skills and knowledge.

C) Happy for being able to contribute to society with your incredible work.

3. Your laptop has stopped working and so you've been on your phone for hours trying to fix the issue. You are actually quite content because:

A) This experience will help you learn a new skill and boost your knowledge.

B) You will be able to fix it yourself.

C) You have a problem to solve – you find the challenge of solving issues quite stimulating, so sacrificing a whole day to do so is no trouble to you.

4. Your closest friend has a problem of some kind and has come to you for help. You:

A) Don't offer any realistic advice – you'd rather focus on the *wants* instead of the *needs*, and advise

them to bite the bullet and do the thing they feel
will make them content emotionally.

B) Use your knowledge to help your friend make a
decision and work with facts.

C) Think practically and offer a logical explanation
to their issue – *You cannot quit your job because you
have the mortgage to think about; it's too risky.*

TYPE 6

**1. Your boss has just assigned you more work, even
though you already are swamped with obligations. You:**

A) Like the challenge to use your knowledge and
abilities to solve the issues and complete the
projects successfully.

B) Don't quite like the fact you have tons of workload, but say nothing.

C) May take a risk and tell your boss that you are
human, not a robot, but you will do so in a funny,
joke-like way, so it doesn't sound like you are
complaining.

**2. You've just spent some time reading about natural
catastrophes. The first thing that comes to your
mind is:**

A) How unfortunate that might be. You immediately start worrying, going through negative scenarios, letting anxiety take over.

B) I must start preparing for such an unfortunate event right away.

C) That is awful, and make a mental reminder that you should do some preparations in the future.

3. Your client has just sent you a causal e-mail that includes a fun introduction before getting to the point. You think:

A) That wasting time with the chit-chat is unnecessary. You wish everyone would just jump straight to the point.

B) It is nice to engage in a casual conversation. Who knows, maybe this person will become your friend one day?

C) That is exactly how an e-mail should be constructed. Just because you're working, it doesn't mean that you should read boring paragraphs.

4. You are planning on selling the house and are on your way to a meeting with your real estate agent. You wish they:

A) Will listen to your wishes carefully, and be clear and to-the-point when presenting solutions and ideas.

B) Will show you that you are in good hands by talking about their long list of clients and other references.

C) Will be casual and personal-oriented to get to know the real you and understand your needs.

TYPE 7

1. Your friend is taking you to their hometown for a fun weekend. You are most excited about:

A) Getting to know new people.

B) The idea of having an adventure.

C) The pleasure of having a weekend off and spending it someplace new.

2. Your boss has told you to come into their office when your lunch break is over. You:

A) Have barely touched your lunch, worried about what they might say to you.

B) Are curious to know what they have to say, but don't give it that much attention.

C) You are not worried because you know you've been at the top of your game at work.

3. **You're entering a party you've been invited to. You are wearing your new dress/pants/shirt. You:**

A) Look at other's people faces to seek approval. You wonder whether they think your new dress/pants/shirt looks good on you.

B) Are optimistic about the night and not concerned with how you look.

C) Walk into the room with confidence. You believe that your charismatic looks appeal to everyone.

4. **Your spouse has just informed you that they have been offered a job transfer to another country. You:**

A) Are a little unsure. The uncertainty of the change is worrisome.

B) Get excited about the opportunity. A breath of fresh air will certainly be good.

C) Immediately start researching the place looking for apartments, so you stay on top of the situation.

360 | NAKED WITH THE ENNEAGRAM

TYPE 8

1. Your friend has taken you as their plus one at a party. You meet new people who crack jokes. To fit in, you:

A) Make some jokes at your expense. Some self-humor always seems to break the ice.
B) Laugh at their jokes and shoot a few fun comments here and there.
C) Are friendly, and might even spice things up with some ironic, dry humor.

2. You have a quick, but very important decision to make. You:

A) Just do it. Moving swiftly isn't a problem for you when the situation requires an energetic and quick response.
B) Make the decision, thinking that you have made a good choice.
C) Need a minute to get your thinking straight. You want to make sure that everyone will be satisfied with the decision.

3. Your boss has just assigned you as a leader of your new project. What makes you content the most?

A) The fact that you get to be dominant because you are not a fan of authority.
B) Having control over the situation so you can be sure the execution will be successful.
C) Feel relieved that you will not have to feel submissive.

4. What is the first thing that comes to your mind when someone talks about *having boundaries?*

A) Pushing them.
B) Setting them.
C) Keeping them firmly.

TYPE 9

1. You have been poorly treated at work for quite some time. Others get the credit, you get the lousy projects. You feel like:

A) Crawling in your bed, putting on a bad Netflix show, and not speaking to anyone.
B) Doing whatever you can to avoid getting into conflict.

C) Struggling between keeping the harmony and unleashing the powerful anger inside.

2. Your friend has just said something that you believe it's quite unfair. You:

A) Have trouble facing them head-on.
B) Remain passive just to keep the peace.
C) Have no problem in being blunt and sharing your opinion.

3. When you are feeling stressed out, what do you think describes you the most?

A) Being cold to other people and somewhat aloof.
B) Usually agreeing to whatever to avoid the conflict, but piling strong feelings deep down.
C) Being stubborn.

4. Imagine you are at your workplace and that your shift is almost over. You would be most satisfied with your day if you have spent it:

A) Sticking to your work routine with the least surprises.
B) In a harmonious environment – good vibe from your colleagues.

C) With a balanced workload – you were able to hold all of the strings together.

SCORING

Now that you have written down your answers, let's calculate the score:

3 or 4 As– That means that you have the previous type (the type on your left) as your dominant wing. If you are a Type One, getting a result of 3 or 4As means that you are 1w9. If you are a Type Two, you are 2w1. If you are Type Three, you are 3w2, and so on.

2 As and 2 Bs – This score means that your wings are mostly balanced, with the previous type slightly overpowering at times. For Type One, that would be – mostly balanced with the wing Nine being more powerful than the wing Two.

2 As and 2 Cs – Congratulations, you have hit the golden middle! Your wings are balancing your personality, and you turn to each of the neighbor types for help.

2 As, 1 B, and 1 C – You have your previous type as your dominant wing. Wing Nine for Type One, wing One for Type Two, wing Three for Type Four, and so on.

3 or 4 Bs – The Bs represent balanced decisions, so if this is your score, then you have already achieved your goal – to balance the wings for the best flight.

2 Bs and 2 Cs – That means that your wings are mostly balanced, with the next type slightly overpowering as a wing. For instance, if you are a Type One, this means that you have slightly balanced wings, with the wing Two being more powerful. If you are Type Two, you are almost balanced, with the wing Three overpowering, and so on.

2 Bs, 1 A, and 1 C – You have balanced wings.

3 or 4 Cs and – You have your next type (the type on your right) as the dominant wing. If you are Type One, then you are 1w2, If you are a Two, you're 2w3, if you're a Three, you're a 3w4, and so on.

2 Cs, 1 A, and 1 B – Your next type is also your dominant wing. Wing Two for Type One, wing Three for Type Two, wing Four for Type Three, and so on.

TEST F

WHICH INSTINCT FORMS YOUR SUBTYPE?

We all have a main personality type we are born with. You can be a One, Two, Five, Nine... You can be a One with a Nine wing. You can be a Nine with an Eight Wing. That is the backbone of who you are, the skeleton of your thoughts, emotions, and actions together. But we are much complex than that. There is also something primal that resides in all of us. Some powerful force that drives our fundamental being, even if we are unaware of it. This force or instinct is separated from our personality, and yet, it lies under the surface and directs the way in which we think, act, feel.

There are three instincts that each of us has:

1. Self-Preservation Instinct **(SP)**
2. Social Instinct **(SO)**
3. Sexual **(One-to-One)** Instinct **(SX)**

But, while the three instincts are always present, only one will be calling the shots. The secondary instinct compliments the one in charge, while the third one is the blind spot – the one we rarely let out of its cage. When the dominant instinct is combined with our Enneagram traits, a new structure called *the Enneagram instinctual subtype* is formed. Given the 9 main Enneatypes and 3 basic instincts, there are 27 Enneagram instinctual subtypes.

To see which of the 3 instinctual subtypes (assuming you've already taken the test and know your main type) is your dominant one, and understand which one is your less and least favorite, I've compiled a detailed test.

So, grab a pen and a piece of paper. Divide the paper into three equal parts – one will be the SP, the second SO, and the third one SX. Under SP, you will be placing the 9 scores you will get on Self-Preservation Test. The SO is where you write the scores for your Social Test, and the SX is for the Sexual scores.

Now, take your time, be brutally honest, and let's find out which instinct drives your type.

SELF-PRESERVATION SUBTYPES

1. You have a very respectful relationship with your body – you stay away from junk food, have enough rest, and hit the gym often.

I totally agree 5
I somewhat agree 4
I'm not sure 3
I somewhat disagree 2
I totally disagree 1

2. Others usually say that you are a very disciplined person, and always finish what you start. You are the I-don't-know-how-he/she-does-it person.

I totally agree 5
I somewhat agree 4
I'm not sure 3
I somewhat disagree 2
I totally disagree 1

3. You often find yourself in a future-worrying mode, trying to make sure that your work and actions will keep you materially secure in the long run.

I totally agree 5
I somewhat agree 4

I'm not sure 3
I somewhat disagree 2
I totally disagree 1

4. When you are stressed out, the thing you neglect the most is your basic needs. You forget to eat, shower, don't care much for your appearance, etc.

I totally agree 5
I somewhat agree 4
I'm not sure 3
I somewhat disagree 2
I totally disagree 1

5. You are not a big fan of taking risks. You would rather just guard what you have managed to achieve in life, even if that means you might lose the opportunity to achieve more.

I totally agree 5
I somewhat agree 4
I'm not sure 3
I somewhat disagree 2
I totally disagree 1

6. You are often concerned about *not having enough supplies*. You always buy more than you need so you can have something extra *just in case*.

I totally agree 5
I somewhat agree 4
I'm not sure 3
I somewhat disagree 2
I totally disagree 1

7. You feel a strong sense of duty to *protect your territory*. You work hard to keep the things and people you have in your life.

I totally agree 5
I somewhat agree 4
I'm not sure 3
I somewhat disagree 2
I totally disagree 1

8. If someone you care about tells you that you have put on some weight, it will only send you to extreme dieting and exercising.

I totally agree 5
I somewhat agree 4
I'm not sure 3
I somewhat disagree 2

I totally disagree 1

9. You are a person who is not a big fan of interpersonal contact and making spontaneous decisions. You'd rather be comfortable in your home – the place you are secure and familiar with.

I totally agree 5
I somewhat agree 4
I'm not sure 3
I somewhat disagree 2
I totally disagree 1

SOCIAL SUBTYPES

1. You feel most energized when you are among a group of people. You find the social connection to be an extremely important part of your life.

I totally agree 5
I somewhat agree 4
I'm not sure 3
I somewhat disagree 2
I totally disagree 1

2. You would choose a double date night out over a movie night with just your partner, in a heartbeat.

I totally agree 5
I somewhat agree 4
I'm not sure 3
I somewhat disagree 2
I totally disagree 1

3. You have numerous acquaintances, and the number seems to be growing by the day.

I totally agree 5
I somewhat agree 4
I'm not sure 3
I somewhat disagree 2
I totally disagree 1

4. You regularly keep in touch with people from high school or the town you grew up in, even if you weren't that close as kids.

I totally agree 5
I somewhat agree 4
I'm not sure 3
I somewhat disagree 2
I totally disagree 1

5. You sometimes do things not because that's what you want, but because that's what you believe the people close to you want.

I totally agree 5
I somewhat agree 4
I'm not sure 3
I somewhat disagree 2
I totally disagree 1

6. You would hate to move to a different country because letting go of all the people you know will be extremely hard.

I totally agree 5
I somewhat agree 4
I'm not sure 3
I somewhat disagree 2
I totally disagree 1

7. You are concerned with what people think of you. Your high social status is what makes you get out of bed most days.

I totally agree 5
I somewhat agree 4
I'm not sure 3
I somewhat disagree 2

I totally disagree 1

8. Your friends always tell you that you know *just the right people*, whether you need to enter a VIP after-party, get last-minute concert tickets, or find someone who can get someone's kid in a fancy kindergarten.

I totally agree 5
I somewhat agree 4
I'm not sure 3
I somewhat disagree 2
I totally disagree 1

9. Being there for your friend is way more important to you than working on a personal project.

I totally agree 5
I somewhat agree 4
I'm not sure 3
I somewhat disagree 2
I totally disagree 1

SEXUAL SUBTYPES

1. You haven't been single since high school (or since you have started dating).

> I totally agree 5
> I somewhat agree 4
> I'm not sure 3
> I somewhat disagree 2
> I totally disagree 1

2. You can flirt your way into anything – whether you need extra dressing for your salad, a free pass to an exhibition, or to cut a line when you're in a hurry.

> I totally agree 5
> I somewhat agree 4
> I'm not sure 3
> I somewhat disagree 2
> I totally disagree 1

3. You don't need tons of friends – you just want to share a deep and intimate connection with the ones you have.

> I totally agree 5
> I somewhat agree 4
> I'm not sure 3

I somewhat disagree 2

I totally disagree 1

4. You are persuasive enough to get other people to do things for you– even on a bad hair day.

I totally agree 5

I somewhat agree 4

I'm not sure 3

I somewhat disagree 2

I totally disagree 1

5. When you talk to people, you feel the need to touch their arm, knee, or put a hand on their shoulder.

I totally agree 5

I somewhat agree 4

I'm not sure 3

I somewhat disagree 2

I totally disagree 1

6. You get fascinated and super attracted to new and unexplored adventures.

I totally agree 5

I somewhat agree 4

I'm not sure 3

I somewhat disagree 2

I totally disagree 1

7. You sometimes feel like you *possess* your partner – you have a strong yearning that forces you to be controlling.

I totally agree 5
I somewhat agree 4
I'm not sure 3
I somewhat disagree 2
I totally disagree 1

8. You don't think you are worthy enough until you can measure up to the people you admire or want to be like.

I totally agree 5
I somewhat agree 4
I'm not sure 3
I somewhat disagree 2
I totally disagree 1

9. You consider yourself a sensitive and romantic person.

I totally agree 5
I somewhat agree 4
I'm not sure 3
I somewhat disagree 2

I totally disagree 1

SCORING

Now that you've written down the scores, you need to simply add them up. Find the total score for each self-preservation, social, and sexual test.

And that's your answer:

Dominant Subtype – The subtype test with the *highest results*

Secondary Subtype – The subtype test with the *lower results*

The Blind Spot – The subtype test with the *lowest results*

It is possible to score the same for both tests, usually for the dominant and secondary subtypes. That just means that your main instincts almost align, or that you rely on each of them equally, just at a different time of your life. If that is the case, please, go back, retake the test and try to be super honest this time. Focus on giving answers that apply to you the most at this moment, for the most accurate results.

FAQ

I've worked really hard to provide you with the most accurate questions for the tests as possible. However, keep in mind that the test isn't created with your unique personality traits in mind. That's just outright impossible. The tests work as a guide to indicate the likelihood of a certain type, but it is possible for you to get misleading results, depending on many factors.

For that reason, when taking the tests make sure that you are:

YOUR OLD SELF — Keep in mind that our Enneagram type is something we are born with. These personality traits are ours since the day we come into this world. However, as we grow older and become aware of which parts of our character are good, and which ones we may be ashamed of or don't like to admit we have, we start

shaping the way we act or feel so we are more *acceptable.*
I'm trying to say that, for more accurate results, pay your
old self a visit. Answer the questions as your younger self
would, preferably around age 20.

ALONE — You may subconsciously shape the results out
of shame or fear of what the person sitting next to you
would think.

IN A GOOD PLACE — You shouldn't be sick, stressed,
exhausted, overwhelmed, or even excited about something when taking the tests. This may force you to choose
an answer in the spur of the moment, which you otherwise wouldn't select. Try to do this when your mind is
calm and you are feeling healthy.

HONEST — And I mean, brutally honest. If you are
sugar-coating or mellowing out the answers, what's the
point of taking the test anyway? The result will not be
accurate. And why wouldn't you be honest? You are
alone, duh!

If you still have some doubts or uncertainties, see if you
can clarify with one of the answers below.

*I've got my top three highest scores, but I cannot identify
myself? What am I doing wrong?*

I recommend that you read the whole book before taking
the tests. The first part of the book contains all of the
information you possibly need to know about the Ennea-

gram, so it only makes sense to educate yourself beforehand, just so you can have a better understanding. For instance, Threes, Sixes, and Nines will probably have a hard time determining their Enneagram types because they cannot identify unless they are connected with others. They sort of *live through other people*, because they need to feel accepted, admired, acknowledged. They might have trouble getting a clear test result because they cannot see them with their own eyes – they need other people to do that for them. But, there are a lot of traits that these three types do not share as well. Learning more about each of the types will help you identify and pinpoint exactly where you stand on the Enneagram. So, check the first part for more accurate results.

I think I share a lot of characteristics with another type. Can I be both?

No! We can only be one type; however, it is not strange that we share a lot of personality traits with other types. In fact, when reading the first part of the book, you will probably find yourself in each of the Nine parts. You may hate mess like One, want to feel loved like Two, want to be professionally successful like Three, feel comfortable when your sad like Four, and so on. We are humans, not robots. We have many different feelings, thoughts, and emotions that change as we grow. But the only thing that stays the same is our underlying motivation. *Why do you do the things you do?* That is what should answer your questions. Think about it. Who doesn't like to be successful, for instance? But that doesn't make you a Three. If you are *doing the things you are doing* so you can be successful and admired by others, then you are a Three. Because *being the best* will be your motivation. So, check with yourself. What is your motivation? That should clarify your doubts.

How come I am Type One when I have a junk drawer, and my closet's not organized?

Some Ones are not affected by mess when it can go unnoticed (like hidden in a drawer). Some Ones couldn't care less about keeping things clean and organized. Just like some Three's can be doubtful, just like Nines can get blunt, angry, and stubborn. That's because there are many shades of the basic types. You have the wings and instinctual subtypes to consider, but also how the type changes when feeling secure or stressed, when in a healthy or unhealthy place. So, if a One is not much into order, they may be leaning toward the criticizing and controlling nature more. That is why you should take all of the tests and then read everything about every aspect of your type in detail.

My results say I'm a certain type, but I feel like I am leaning toward a different type? How can I be sure?

Read the questions more carefully, and try to be more honest about the results. Sometimes, when two types are connected in a way – like Five taking on the good traits of Eight when in a good place – the results can be tricky to decipher. If this doesn't help, then read the description of the types more carefully. Or take the wing and subtype tests for both Five and Eight, and see if this helps.

Is it possible to score evenly or have a very close result?

Yes and no! For the types, you cannot share the same score because you cannot be two types at the same time. If this was the case with you, try to read the descriptions for the types or re-test tomorrow. Perhaps something is affecting the result without you even knowing? As for the instinctual subtypes, it is possible to have a nearly identical result. That means that you switch between the two instinctual subtypes depending on what you are going through, but still, you should only have one when it comes to your main instinct. No matter how small the difference in the score, the one that takes the lead dominates.

If all else fails, just let the person who knows you best take the test for you. Sometimes, we subconsciously fear letting ourselves down, so we give answers that are not really true for us.

I'VE TESTED

NOW WHAT?

If you've taken all 6 of the tests, congratulations! You have officially discovered not only your Enneagram type but the overall structure that shapes your personality, as well.

Now that you know your type, dominant wing (or balanced!), main and secondary subtypes, the only thing left for you to do is simply jump back to the first part of this book and interpret your results. You know, like finding out just how controlling Ones are, or where you are as a sexual Four with a dominant wing Three. All things Enneagram about your personality are explained well there, so you should have smooth sailing.

So, have a Kleenex box nearby (there might be some sobbing), pour yourself a tall glass of wine (trust me, you'll need it), and get ready to introduce yourself to the real you.

I'd love to hear all about your self-discovery! Leave a review and let me know. Your feedback is always greatly appreciated!

Happy self-searching,

Adriana

FREE GIFTS

To say thank you for buying my book, I would like to give you:

- A **Cheatsheet with a Summary of all the Enneagram Types** — to make remembering and understanding even easier, you can always come back to it in times of need. All the types' main personality traits, worst fear, heart's desire, biggest sin & more at a glance. You can also print it out and pin it somewhere in your home or office where you'll easily see it.
- A high-resolution, printable **Daily Affirmations and Transformations sheet for each Enneagram Type** — to help you quickly recognize old patterns and replace them with a boost of

transforming energy through your affirmations for your specific type. Pin them anywhere you can see them daily, at home or at the office; put them on a wall in a nice frame or even save them as a desktop background.

- An **Excel file to automatically calculate the Enneagram test results** — the first test (Test A) is the base test and has the most questions. To make things easier for you, I created an Excel file where you can insert your scores for Test A and the results will be automatically calculated. There is a specific tab for each test where you can fill in your answers and scores to keep a record of your results.

- A **Summary of the book *Naked With the Enneagram*** — in this pocketbook version you can go over the "CliffsNotes" of the book without going into much detail. Use it as you see fit. For example, as a short read reminder of the complete book, or share the link as a gift to a friend who's not quite ready to embark on the complete book journey, or whatever else helps you.

- High-resolution, printable **Images from the book *Naked With the Enneagram*** — to have a better experience while reading the white & black version of the book all the color images are accessible to view online, download or print. Choose what works best for you.

DOWNLOAD HERE:

www.NakedEnneagram.com/freebies

WHAT DO YOU THINK?

A HUGE THANK YOU for reading *Naked with the Enneagram!*

You could have picked up other books about the Enneagram, but you took a chance to check out this one. I sincerely hope it has been rewarding for you.

Could you help? You have the power to make this book fly, or fail. This book is completely self-published. That means there's not a big, powerful publishing company promoting it. Readers like you are supporting and funding its growth.

Reviews from readers like you are the main metric that people will use to judge a book's content. Your review will help other readers find out what the book is all about. If you enjoyed your Enneagram journey, please take one minute to tell other readers (and me) about it! Every single review has a huge impact on others' willingness to read a book, and if this book helped you in any way, you can help someone else by spreading the word. The impact and reach of this book are up to you.

If it helps you, use the following questions as prompts:

What is your Enneagram type and how do you feel about it?

What part of the book did you like best?

How did the book help you?

Why do you think the book would benefit others?

What improvements would you like to see?

I'd be forever grateful if you left a few thoughts. I read every single review and take them very seriously. **It will be one minute for you and a lifetime of help for me!** You can leave a review by going to your Amazon orders or scanning the QR code below.

Plus if you leave a review in the first 15 days after buying the book, I'll create a printable artwork for you with your favorite quote from the book. Just send me the quote you like along with the copy of the review you posted:

www.nakedenneagram.com/contact

PS: Please don't be brutal if you find any errors in punctuation, spelling, or grammar, but do tell me at the link above.

Connect with Adriana on Instagram or Facebook:

Instagram: @naked_enneagram

Facebook: @NakedEnneagram

RECOMMENDATIONS AND RESOURCES

Would You Like to Know More? You can learn a lot more about the Enneagram or personal development in my other future books. You'll have the opportunity to get my new books for free or at heavy discounts, enter giveaways, and receive other valuable emails from me.

Sounds good? You can sign up here https://www.subscribepage.com/nakedenneagram or by scanning the QR code below.

Would you like more help to go deeper into your Enneagram journey right now? *Stephanie Barron Hall* from Ninetypes.co is a certified Enneagram coach that would love to be by your side in your Enneagram journey and answer any questions you might have.

Here's Steph describing briefly the process of a typing session:

"My conversation-based approach blends conversation, reflection, and insight to put the power back in your hands. As an impartial observer, I'll guide you through core motivations, core fears, and focuses of attention to help you find what truly resonates with you. At the end of our session, we'll recap some thoughts on your type, and then I'll send you away with some direction to continue reflecting. After our session, I'll send over some resources for further insight. The goal here is to equip you with the tools you need to not just understand your type but actually apply the Enneagram knowledge you gain. Doing the growth work during the typing process will help you integrate helpful practices throughout your Enneagram journey. Talk to you soon! With love, Steph."

Don Richard Riso and Russ Hudson (1999) – *The Wisdom of the Enneagram: The Complete Guide to Psychological and Spiritual Growth for the Nine Personality Types.* Bantam

Baron, R. and Wagele E. (1994) – *The Enneagram Made Easy Discover the 9 Types of People.* HarperOne

Chestnut B. (2013) – *The Complete Enneagram: 27 Paths to Greater Self-Knowledge.* She Writes Press

The Enneagram Institute – *How the Enneagram System Works* - https://www.enneagraminstitute.com/how-the-enneagram-system-works

The Enneagram Institute – *The Enneagram Type Combinations* - https://www.enneagraminstitute.com/the-enneagram-type-combinations

The Enneagram at Work – *Nine Enneagram Types* - https://theenneagramatwork.com/nine-enneagram-types

Booth, J. (2018) – *This is the One Thing to Know About Your Enneagram Personality Type* - https://www.bustle.com/p/what-do-the-different-enneagram-types-mean-theyre-extremely-specific-8538878

The Enneagram in Business (2010) – *Enneagram Theory: Enneagram Wings* - https://theenneagraminbusiness.com/theory/enneagram-theory-enneagram-wings/

Paulk, S. (2020) – *The Enneagram at Work – Which Number Are You?* - https://www.success.com/the-enneagram-at-work/

Daniels, D. – *The 45 Combinations of Enneagram Relationships* - https://drdaviddaniels.com/relationships-intimacy/enneagram-types-in-relationship/

Rob, F. – *Levels of development* -

http://fitzel.ca/enneagram/levels.html

Credits for a part of the vector graphics to slidesgo / Freepik: http://www.freepik.com

Credits for a part of the vector graphics to https://www.vecteezy.com/free-vector/flat-character

Made in the USA
Las Vegas, NV
10 May 2023

71838726R00223